The

The Youngest Drover

*A true story about growing up
on a cattle drive*

RON CARTER

HARBOUR BOOKS

Copyright © 1994 by Ron Carter

Published by:

Harbour Books
147 Armstrong
Claremont, CA 91711

Library of Congress Catalog Number 94-079565

Paperback ISBN: 0-9643672-0-3: $14.95
Hardcover ISBN: 0-9643672-1-1: $19.95

Design and production: Barbara J. Ciletti
Jacket/cover illustrations: Cathy Morrison, Big Chief Graphics
Typesetting: Westype Publishing Services, Boulder, Colorado
Printing: Community Press, Provo, Utah

10 9 8 7 6 5 4 3 2 1

The
Sculpture

The preceding sculpture was created by Earl Wesley Bascom from photographs and descriptions of Melvin William Carter, who is young Henry McEwen in the book, The Youngest Drover. The likeness is striking. The sculpture was created by Mr. Bascom after reading the book, when he realized how much of the Old West was captured in the true story.

Curiously, Mr. Bascom spent much of his youth in Raymond, Alberta, Canada where the story takes place, and knew Melvin William Carter, and his older brother, Elmer, who is Elmer McEwen in the book.

He was born in 1906 and in his lifetime has been a world rodeo champion and an internationally renowned sculptor. His bronze works are found in the Royal Society of Arts in London, England, in the collections of kings, presidents and dozens of art museums the world over.

Mr. Bascom resides at Bascom Ranches, 15669 Stoddard Wells Road, Victorville, California, 92392.

INTRODUCTION

I cannot identify the time I heard the first story from my father. I only know that listening to them was as native to me as knowing him. I heard them at home, in the car, or at work in my family's livestock business. Some he told me in the fields, carrying shotguns while we hunted. They were simple stories of his growing years. I look back now and realize I just took it for granted that everyone had a dad who was raised on a cow ranch in the vast, wide open prairies of Southern Alberta, Canada. And I assumed my father's stories were of events that were fairly common in those days.

The house he provided for my brothers, sisters, and myself was modern. We always had the necessities and a few luxuries. We also had his stories about trudging fifty feet to an outhouse in fifty-five below zero temperatures, hauling water from a well from which you had to break six inches of ice at the bottom of the well to get it, bootlegging wheat in huge wagons, down across the international border to Cut Bank, Montana. And one time, getting lost in a blizzard so blinding he and his father couldn't see the lead horses. Those horses stopped and wouldn't budge. Climbing from the wagon, the men found the horses leaning against a barbed wire fence—where no fence should have been. They had turned in the blizzard, and except for that fence, would have continued out into wide open prairie in the wrong direction, all night. He had hunted coyotes for four dollars and run wild horses in from the prairie. He was eight years old when he broke his first horse and was 14 when he won second money in a rodeo. He told me of the time he shot a coyote at 582 paces, braided his first four-strand rawhide lariat, and how he woke to the crashing of shots at a family of wolves.

In January of 1923, when he was barely fifteen, he had gone in the company of nine other men to drive twenty-eight hundred head of cattle to Sweetgrass, Montana, in an effort to save what they could of more than five thousand that were starving and freezing to death. These men often were sustained by their humor and the unwavering support of their women in these tough times. The women, standing firm to take all the punishment a harsh, unbending nature could hand out while they supported their men and raised their children. In those days, in that place, a woman's losses came right out of her bones in the children they buried at birth, or within days after, often never knowing the cause. Few of the women ever saw more than grinding poverty.

As a grown man with eight children of my own, I began to realize what my father had told me. I saw that what was native to me was not just a typical family story. I began digging into family records, reading diaries, checking history books. The cattle drive from Raymond, Alberta, Canada, in 1923 appeared as an event in a large factual account of Southern Alberta. Alma Miner Carter's name showed up, along with Melvin William Carter, my father and grandfather, respectively. I found an ancient photograph of the small, two room frame home on the prairie where my father was raised with his six brothers and sisters, not counting Darwin who was stillborn.

I called my cousin Helen, who still lives in Alberta, and we exchanged letters about how it is, and how it was sixty years ago.

I realized that those men and women—whatever they suffered and lost—were survivors.

Suddenly I knew I wanted to perpetuate these stories. So I wrote it for myself, my kids and grandkids, and for all readers who enjoy discovering the real heroes in the making of America.

Chapter One

I wanted to go on the cattle drive more than anything in my life, and I knew my father wouldn't let me do it. Standing in the bitter January cold with the familiar sounds and pungent smells of more than four thousand cattle and two hundred horses all around me, I knew I *had* to get some distance between me and the little nothing of a town called Raymond in the southern end of the Province of Alberta, Canada.

The sound of bawling cattle was a part of life I loved, but I couldn't take one more day of the stubborn, blind set of mind my dad had come into lately. His criticism was making just being alive pure misery for me, and I couldn't take the thought of living with the dull monotony of the ranch and Raymond for one more season.

I had to prove to father that he was wrong about me! He had no cause, no right, to be after me all the time about things that didn't mean nothing. I wasn't the no-account worthless young punk he seemed to think I was!

The men who would decide about the drive and choose the crew were gathered near the herd. There was David Baker, owner of the biggest cattle operation in the whole Province of Alberta, his foreman Charles MacDonald with his thick Scottish accent, my father, Frank Knight, and some of the other owners and representatives from ranches covering hundreds of square miles from

McGrath to Lethbridge to Cardston. They stood on the ground, their horses waiting nearby, stamping their booted feet against the cold, spurs jingling. They looked like small teepees in their heavy woolen or buffalo-robe coats. They wore their hats low and had scarves wrapped around the lower parts of their faces against the freezing cold.

These men had been with us since we started nearly a week ago. Each morning just over sixty of us cowhands from all the ranches had rolled out of stiff, frost-covered blankets and tarps before dawn in the bitter Canadian January to gather all the beef animals we could find. They had been running free on the vast unfenced prairie since early in September. Working through the brush in all the draws and coulees and gullies all day had been slow, tough, tedious, freezing work, and we had gone back to our blankets after dark dog tired.

None of us needed to be told we were all in the worst kind of trouble. What started out to be a dry summer was a full drought by August that stunted the range grasses. Going into the fall, stockmen had looked up from the prairie every day to the heavens, hoping for rains that would put some strength back into the grass before the cold settled in and stopped the growth entirely. The rain didn't come. What sparse and weak grass there was died, preventing the cattle from putting on their usual heavy cover of fat for the winter. The frost started in early October, which meant there wouldn't be any more rain. The cattle were in bad shape and the stockmen became increasingly nervous and edgy, short tempered.

The first cold snap hit us in late October. The old-timers started spending three days at a time out looking, judging how long the frayed, scarce prairie grass would last for winter feed. They began sifting through the draws and gullies, moving the cattle out where they could see them, judging whether they would last through a tough winter. They came back silent and sullen, with dark expressions on their faces, mouths clamped shut, saying nothing.

By late December they quit going out in the snow to look. In their eyes quiet desperation mixed with raw fear. If we didn't get rid of half the cattle within just days, all we would find on the open range come spring would be bleaching bones and rotting hides, scattered on prairie so badly overgrazed it wouldn't recover for years.

We had to get half the cattle off the range to try to save the other half, and save the range too. But what do you do with about four thousand head of half-wild range cattle on the Canadian prairie in the middle of January when you have to get rid of them? Shoot them? Try to sell them? To whom? Where? Would the price be so low there'd be no point in trying to get them to market? How much money would we need to get out of the sale to restock later, when the grass came back?

We didn't know the answers, but one thing we did know. They had to go, and to accomplish that, we had to gather them. So we did. We had finished the roundup this morning and the tally this afternoon. We had 4,296 head of poor-quality cattle, from heifers and steers to range bulls and brood cows; the feeder calves from last year's crop had been cut out at the roundup earlier in the year and shipped to feedyards. The brood cows weren't due to start dropping this year's calf crop for another seventy-five days.

The cattle were humped up against the cold with their heads down, the sorriest-looking bunch I could remember seeing. Their hipbones stuck out so far you could hang your hat on them, and you could count their ribs at a hundred yards.

In my own mind I figured we should cut out the brood cows and the range bulls and keep them here as foundation stock to rebuild the herds. It was the heifers and steers we had to get rid of. The only way I could figure doing that was to make a cattle drive south, down over the Milk River Ridge across the international border into the United States—to Sweetgrass, Montana, where there was a railhead with cattle pens and a railroad siding for loading cattle. We could ship them to the market in Chicago. But I had never heard or even dreamed that cattle in these numbers could be moved from Raymond to Sweetgrass in the icy grip of a Canadian winter. Not one man on the roundup had ever heard of it either, but it was in all our minds every minute we were awake. We didn't mention it out loud because it was such a new, awesome notion; but we were all silently making our best guess as to whether it could be done. Desperate men take desperate gambles, and we were clear past the point of being desperate. Either we pulled this off or the whole south end of the Province of Alberta folded and quit.

And now it all had come down to what this little knot of men was saying and deciding. They had gathered late each afternoon for the past six days, talking, arguing, listening, letting their minds settle. Now the time for talking was past. They had to make the decisions that would save us or ruin us. They were scared clear to their bones; you could see it in their eyes.

I couldn't stand not knowing what they were deciding. I reined in not far from them and dismounted just within earshot, standing with my gray between me and them. I draped the reins over my left arm, hooked the left stirrup over the saddlehorn, and stood there in the freezing, dry air of the late afternoon trying to look busy with the latigo on my saddle like I wasn't listening. The dark blue wool scarf mother had knitted was wrapped around my neck and up over my nose and mouth. My wide-brimmed, high-crowned, sweat-stained black hat was pulled down almost to my eyebrows for warmth. My heavy leather bullhide chaps helped turn the prairie wind, but after spending six days and nights on the open range, with temperatures that reached thirty-nine degrees below zero—and two of those days with winds that penetrated my thick, heavy wool coat—I believed I would never be warm again. With leather-gloved fingers that were numb from the cold I fumbled to pull the locking loop tight on the cinch, straining to hear anything that would let me know what these men were going to decide.

They called my older brother Elmer over, and after talking awhile with Charlie MacDonald, Elmer nodded and reined his horse around. He loped away from them, toward the fire, vapor trailing from the nostrils of his gelding at every stride.

My father glanced over at me as Charlie MacDonald turned his head to study me and my big gray horse. Then the talk continued, intentionally kept low, muffled by the scarves. It looked like their discussion might be including me. I didn't even dare to hope what that might mean.

I knew Elmer shouldn't make such a drive. In the summer he had come down with a fever that ran his temperature up to 105 degrees. He was out of his head for almost three days, seeing things that weren't there and talking about crazy things, some true, some pure fantasy. We kept wet, cold towels on him, but he didn't get better. Mother was sure he was going to die, so father took him to Calgary to a doctor. He had undulant fever, or brucellosis, caused by drinking unboiled milk from a diseased cow. We knew about milk fever, but "brucellosis" was a new term to us. It finally began to leave him and he started to improve, but he wasn't back to his full strength. The last six days of roundup left him weak. I figured the men had told him just now to head back home and stay down until his strength came back. If Elmer couldn't go . . .

Were they considering sending me on the cattle drive? That seemed nearly impossible. I was just twenty-two days past my fifteenth birthday. I wasn't large. I stood about five feet eight inches and weighed about 140 pounds. My dark hair and brown eyes gave me something of an older look. My features were regular, although I always thought I had a little too much nose. No one had ever accused me of being handsome. But still, when I got my blood up for something, there was a certain set to my jaw and flash in my eyes that made people look twice, even at fourteen and fifteen.

Still quietly working with the cinch strap, I held my breath so I could hear better. I only caught a few words. I heard MacDonald use the word "drover," rolling the r's off his tongue in that thick Scottish brogue. I knew he called his trailhands "drovers;" he was one of the few I had ever heard use that word. I heard the words "too young" and "school." It had to be me they were talking about. I was the youngest one on the roundup. I had been pulled out of school because they needed me. It *had* to be me.

School. I could hardly stand the thought of going back to that one-room slab-sided building where all the kids within twenty-five miles gathered every day. I wasn't the biggest or oldest, but I was sure the boredest. Learning things came easy to me, and after listening to Mrs. Coltrin every winter for eight years, I knew every word she was going to speak before she spoke it. About ten days ago she had asked me to repeat the alphabet, mostly for the benefit of the younger kids. It was about the tenth time she had done it. Just to be smart, I repeated it as fast as I could, backwards, starting with Z and ending with A. Doing it backwards was just something I had worked out in my mind from boredom.

Mrs. Coltrin stood there in shock, thinking I had done it just to insult her. I didn't care. There was darn little else to do while she was teaching the first and second graders how it went. When father heard about it, I got a going-over about being a smart-aleck know-it-all.

I saw my father shake his head. If he had anything to say about this drive, I figured there was no chance.

Lately he and I hadn't been saying much to each other, and the few words we did speak were about as warm as the wind now freezing my booted feet. I just couldn't understand how he could be so stubborn and so dumb at the same time about some things. It seemed like he got real mad lately at just about anything I did. I figured it was just because he was too set in his ways, like old folks sometimes get. I was the youngest of the six children, and it just figured that with him past fifty, he had lost all patience. He didn't understand that the world had changed from when he was a kid, or even from when he raised my older brothers and sisters. They were all married now except for Elmer; he and I were the only ones still at home. I didn't mind work, not even hard work, but it seemed like I could never do it well enough to satisfy Jacob McEwen. He just kept harping at me—I wasn't serious enough; I didn't understand that life was a pretty tough proposition; I had to get some serious thoughts into my head. It seemed like it never stopped.

I couldn't make him understand that this was 1923, not 1890. The old ways he insisted were right had to give ground to the new ways. Automobiles were all over in Calgary now, and there were even a few in Raymond, the little town nearest our ranch. I had seen a grain combine that harvested wheat so fast it could finish in one day what it took six of us a week to do—tying the shocks and throwing them on the horse-drawn flatbed wagon to be hauled to the barn for thrashing by hand. There were towns, some right in the Province of Alberta, that were getting up to fifteen and twenty thousand people, with modern ways of living that were a long way ahead of anything in Raymond. There were a lot of good jobs in towns and cities where a man could make a mark for himself if he could just get there and get the hang of city living. But my father couldn't understand.

I thought he drank too much, too. I had gotten into some pretty bad arguments with him about that and just about everything else. I couldn't stand him always harping about doing things *his* way, and never listening to *my* ideas. If I took longer doing something than he thought I should, or if I put it off until later, I was lazy. After supper it seemed I did nothing but sit in the house with nothing to do except look at the walls and get lectured. We weren't even playing checkers any more, and that was something we had done on those long winter evenings at home ever since I could remember. I had gotten so I could beat anybody in the family. I even started using three less men than the others just to make it a closer game. Once father had taken me to Chance's Pool Hall in town and challenged J. W. Brewerton to play me. I won, and word got out pretty fast that the ten-year-old McEwen kid had beaten J. W. Brewerton. From then on people saw me as the local authority on checkers. I didn't see it like that. It just came natural after watching father and all the older kids play it ever since I could walk.

I had gotten into some bad arguments with father about how he treated mother, too. He was always respectful, but I figured she had earned a better life than she was getting six miles from town in a two-room handmade unpainted frame house. We'd lived with dirt floors until five years ago when we put a plank floor in. I criticized him for what she was putting up with. I told mother she ought to stand up and tell him herself, just once. She just looked sad and turned away.

It was no secret I was thinking of leaving home so I wouldn't have to put up with his stubborn mule-headedness and his never-ending lectures any more.

As I thought about all this, father and the other men began to move around. They had agreed on what they were going to do. I could hardly wait for them to call us all in and let us know.

When Charlie MacDonald turned toward me and motioned with his hand for me to come over, I couldn't believe it. I looked at my father for any signal that would tell me what they wanted. I got none. He'd keep me home just out of spite if for no other reason.

I nodded to Charlie MacDonald, doubled the last eighteen inches of the cinch strap back through the locking loop, and jerked it tight, dropping the stirrup and fender back down from the saddlehorn. With the reins in my hand I walked the gray over to the men.

"Yer father has a few cattle in this gather," said Charlie, "and yer older brother isn't recovered from the milk fever." His face was expressionless, noncommittal. He rolled his *r*'s so hard it seemed like they started and ended every word he used. I had to listen real careful to be sure I got it all. I nodded, my eyes boring into his, and waited for him to continue.

"He ought to have a rep go along, and he also feels responsible for doin' his share to support this drive, which means he intends sendin' a drover with us. He can't leave yer brother in charge at the ranch because he's still sick, and yer mother has all she can do to nurse him and keep ahead of the work at the house. So yer father has to stay at the ranch. That leaves you."

My heart stopped. Father had lost his mind. I was going on this cattle drive!

Charlie shifted his feet. "We'll be gone nearly two weeks, lad. Once ye leave here there's no turnin' back until we finish. Ye have a little idea of what ye'll be gettin' into from the last six days. But I got a duty to tell ye some other things. Besides the cold there's the chance of no water part of the way and of accidents that can cripple or kill. We're startin' out in the worst part of the winter, and bad weather—maybe a blizzard—can stop us. If it's bad enough it can take the whole herd, maybe some of us with it. Or we could get caught in a chinook and end up in mud clear up to our horses' bellies. While it ain't likely, it's also possible somethin' will start these animals runnin', and if they stampede for any distance at all there's goin' to be some of them or some of us, or both, get hurt. Maybe killed. So Henry, my only question is, do ye think ye can handle it?"

I didn't hesitate. "Yes sir, Mr. MacDonald, I can handle it." I said it quietly, without moving or changing expression.

Inside I was shouting "Can I handle it? I can handle it with one hand. I can handle it asleep. I can handle it unconscious or dead. Of course I can handle it, you old buzzard. Open the chute and let 'er buck. When do we start?"

He looked at me for several seconds. No, he didn't look *at* me. That old Scot looked *clear through* me before he spoke again. "There's one thing I must warn ye about, lad. Yer the youngest drover I ever took on fer a drive like this. I can't give ye any allowance fer yer age, even if I wanted to. Ye'll have to take my orders without question and do what yer told. There's no place fer hardheads and smart alecks on a cattle drive. Do ye understand what I'm tellin' ye, lad?"

"I won't need allowances, Mr MacDonald. I'll pull my weight."

"Tomorrow we cut out all the steers and heifers. We're goin' to take them to Sweetgrass to the railhead and load them onto railroad cars for the Chicago market. We'll hold them here tonight, so go home now and show up here at daybreak tomorrow when we settle all this with the ranchers. We'll spend tomorrow sortin' out the heifers and steers. The followin' mornin' we start southeast over the Milk River Ridge. Ye'll receive the same wages as the rest of us, and gettin' any wages at all depends on what we can get fer these animals at the Chicago stockyards. Get yer gear and necessaries and be back here ready in the mornin'."

"Yes, sir. I'll be here."

I waited for a minute to see if he was finished. He turned and walked back toward his horse. My father had already mounted and was walking his horse back to the fire.

I don't know how I controlled myself. Inside I threw my hat in the air and howled like old Lobo the wolf. But on the outside I calmly turned to the gray, tossed the off rein up over his neck, raised my left foot to the stirrup and swung up. I started over toward the fire. Father saw me coming and turned his horse toward home. I silently fell in beside him. I wanted to ask him everything that had been said, how it was decided I was to go on the drive, but I didn't know how. I just kept the gray moving beside him, wanting to talk, wondering why I couldn't.

Father motioned to Elmer, who fell in beside us. We rode in silence, each with his own thoughts. We were going to be busy getting me ready to leave by four in the morning.

Chapter Two

       With the night of preparation behind me, I reined the gray around in the predawn darkness for just a minute to take a last look back at the house. I sat there in the saddle, vapor clouds floating upward from the muzzle of the horse. My scarf was wound over my nose and anchored inside my heavy coat, and I was breathing the frigid air pretty shallow to keep it from freezing my lungs.

       The morning star was just fading in the east. In the near-total blackness, the kerosene lamplight shining through the kitchen window laid a long shaft of yellow brightness on the frozen ground, reflecting off the glittering frost crystals, illuminating the outhouse and the shed to the south and east.

       I had expected to be full of anticipation and excitement about the cattle drive, but I wasn't. There was no peace in my mind as I sat there on the gray, my brow knitted down, looking back at my home with my people inside. I was struggling to sort out why I felt such a pull to be there with them, all the while knowing I could hardly stand being around my father, or this ranch, or the unpainted, ugly little town.

       Lost in my troubled thoughts, I turned the gray's nose away from home and eastward toward the fading morning star. Giving the lead rope on the sorrel backup horse a gentle tug, I urged the gray into a trot. The three of us—the gray, the sorrel mare, and me, carrying all our gear for the drive—covered half a mile before I pulled them down to a steady walk. Don't sweat them in this kind of cold, I reminded myself.

My thoughts kept going back over the happenings of last night and early this morning, and even back to last summer. I had a nagging suspicion I was missing something, and it just wouldn't let go. Now, with just me and the horses alone in a silent, frozen world, with six miles to cover, maybe I had time to sort it out. At least some of it.

I started back through it a piece at a time. When I came home yesterday, I was sure Elmer would be edgy because he was sick and couldn't make the drive; and I figured he'd still be mad at me for the ruckus we got into last September before the freeze set in. Mother had said how nice it would be to have some gooseberries for a pie, so Elmer and I mounted up that Saturday and went out onto the prairie to get some. I rode my gray and Elmer rode a little two-year-old green broke gelding that he liked. We were traveling slow and easy because Elmer was still weak. Picking the berries wasn't hard work, so we soon had our buckets about full.

Elmer is one of the best I know for handling horses, but when it came time to go home he pulled a trick that wasn't like him at all. He got his foot into the stirrup to step up onto the little gelding, and then absent-mindedly reached for the cheek strap on the split-ear bridle to hold the horse's head so he wouldn't buck. The problem was he had the berry bucket in the same hand. When he grabbed the cheek strap, the bucket swung up under the horse's head and smacked him on the jawbone. The gelding didn't know why he was getting cracked on the jaw, but he sure took it poorly. He exploded straight into the air and came down ready to fight anything in general and Elmer in particular. He cut some of the fanciest capers I ever saw. Elmer couldn't bear to let go of the bucket and lose all the berries he'd picked, and he couldn't let the horse learn it could win by tearing up the countryside, and he couldn't get his leg over the horse with all the acrobatics going on, so there Elmer hung. He couldn't get clear on, and he wouldn't get clear off, and he wouldn't let go of the berry bucket. With every jump, the bucket swung back up to smack the horse, and the horse started for the clouds all over again. Elmer soon lost all the berries, and he wound up flat on his back. I finally caught the horse, which was a real job, considering he was heading for Mexico about as hard as he could run. I think he wanted to be somewhere else as quick as he could, where he wasn't going to get smacked on the jaw every jump by something he couldn't see, for no reason he could figure out.

Well, it struck me as probably the funniest thing I had seen all year and I started to laugh. Elmer took strong exception to my notions of funny. When he got the horse settled down he gave me a real good big-brother preachment. I ignored his brotherly advice and just kept grinning, which made him all the madder.

I chuckled half the way home. When we unsaddled, I was still smiling, even though I knew Elmer was trying real hard to keep murder out of his mind. Walking across the corral after we had racked our saddles in the shed, I busted out laughing at him again. This time Elmer lost his hold on his temper. He was still sick and weak from the fever, and mad at himself, and feeling foolish.

He grabbed my shoulder and yelled at me. I laughed in his face. He took a swing at me, his fist grazing my cheek. He was bigger than me by quite a bit, so there wasn't much of a chance I could fight him. On his next swing I ducked. My back was against the snubbing post in the middle of the corral, so when I ducked his fist banged into the post. He grabbed his hand and sort of hunched down, and I knew the ruckus was over.

At supper that night father asked what had happened to my cheek. I told him a horse had kicked me. He looked at Elmer's swollen, useless hand for a moment. "I suppose the horse kicked you too, Elmer." Elmer only nodded.

Elmer hadn't gotten over that yet. I thought he was down on me for good.

But last night, while I was getting my gear together out in the shed in the yellow glow of the kerosene lamp, he showed up with his rawhide lariat. A good hand-braided, four-strand rawhide lariat is something coveted by almost anyone who figures himself to be a cowhand. I never saw one break in my whole life, no matter what the load on it. They hold a loop better than anything else, and are just stiff enough to throw hard in the wind. It isn't easy to come by one of those lariats. You have to carefully cure and scrape about four prime beef hides, cut each one into a continuous eighty-foot strip about a quarter of an inch wide, soak them soft, and then round braid them without any flaws. I had started one last summer, working on it every chance I got, but it wasn't finished.

I wanted a good rawhide lariat for this cattle drive so bad I could taste it. In the shed, I had just tied my store-bought hemp lariat to my saddle when Elmer walked in. He wasn't too good with words and didn't seem to know what to say. He just handed his lariat to me and looked at me for a minute before he turned to go. Now how do you figure that?

"Elmer, I . . ." I didn't know quite what to say, either. He paused for a second but went on out the door and back to the house.

And then mother. I had laid out three thick wool blankets on the heavy canvas tarp and was about to roll up my bedroll when she showed up at the shed. She walked over to the saddle, lifted the cover of one saddlebag, and dropped in a brown wrapper filled with her biscuits. That was a real treat.

But it was what she said that I couldn't get out of my head. "Henry, while you're gone, think about Jacob. He only wants what's good for you. He's had so many disappointments in his life he's about worn out with them. Think about him and try to understand. He doesn't mean to be hard on you. He just knows how hard life and its changes can be. He tries to understand the way things are going, with motorcars and electric lights and new notions and all, but it's hard for him. And me. Try to understand him."

Then she cheered up a little and gave me the usual lecture about staying away from strong drink and women. I promised her I would. I meant it. It was hard for me to not do what mother asked, no matter what it was.

If father had seen tough times, mother had seen worse. My older sister Ferl had told me it seemed like a light had gone out inside my mother when they buried my next older brother, the one between me and Elmer, just a few days after he was born. They named him Darwin and went through a full funeral before they buried him in the Raymond cemetery. Ferl said that after mother saw the tiny casket lowered into the small hole in the vast, rolling prairie, her eyes lost their light, just went kind of blank and stayed that way a long time.

After mother left, I finished checking the hooves and ankles on the gray and the sorrel. I was just straightening up when Jacob walked into the shed. In his hand was the old .45-70 Springfield breach-loading rifle. He leaned it against my saddle, lifted the flap on the saddlebag, and dropped twenty bullets inside.

He had told Charlie he would send the rifle. Charlie was bringing a .30-30 Winchester repeater and a double-barreled shotgun along in the chuckwagon. The Springfield was close to five feet long and weighed about a country ton. It loaded through a breach door that you opened and then snapped closed after you slipped in a shell that was about three or four inches long. The rear sight had an elevator that you could set up to two thousand yards, which was no exaggeration of how far that old cannon would shoot. Rumor had it that if you put the right angle on it, the bullet would go until it wore out before it hit the ground. Some said if you were going to shoot a real long shot you should salt the bullet, so the meat wouldn't spoil before you got to it the next day.

I knew my father wanted to say something, and I knew I wanted to say something, but neither one of us knew how to do it or what to say. It was sort of awkward, embarrassing, for just a second. Then Jacob simply said, "Remember who you are. Do your job." That was all I got. I watched his heavy coat disappear in the dark as he walked out the shed door and back to the house.

Standing there in the yellow lamplight, vapor drifting up from my breath, I tried to sort out my recollections of the past couple of years when things had started getting testy between us. I was certain *I* hadn't changed much. But *he* seemed to get more set in his ways and his notions with every passing day. The past year, I couldn't do *anything* right.

Every day of my life, I had to hear him go through it again: I didn't do my work at the ranch right, and I wouldn't do my schoolwork. I couldn't handle my money, and I hardly ever had a serious thought about anything. I never kept care of my clothes, and I wouldn't do my chores without being lectured first. All I wanted to do was run around, getting involved in nonsense ʾ ɩh the wrong crowd of trash in town, talking about cars and cities, getting into things that would be my ruination.

To me, that was dumb. I did my share and I did it pretty good. The guys I ran around with on the few occasions when I got to town were just the kids from other ranches. They weren't bad kids. Why couldn't he see something good in me? I just figured that *something* I did must be right.

Why couldn't Jacob see what this prairie had done to him and mother? Why couldn't he see what it would do to the rest of us? I *knew* there were better things to do than live and work fifty years and then die on this prairie with nothing more than you had when you were born. No hopes, no dreams, and no change—doing on the last day of your life what you had done every other day.

It had really gotten bad between me and Jacob last fall, the day we ended roundup. Every fall, cowboys from nearly a hundred miles in every direction rounded up all the cattle we could find and gathered them in one big herd. Calves were cut, notched, and branded; feeders would go to the feedyards; and old cows and bulls would be shipped to the slaughterhouse.

After we finished, a lot of us younger guys headed for Calgary about 120 miles north for the rodeo. It was just part of the round-up. Calgary wasn't much, but there was a rodeo arena at the edge of town where for a couple of days people from all over southern Alberta gathered for some rough, good-humored fun before the heavy Canadian winter closed in. Despite being small and home-made, the Calgary Stampede had produced some of the best cowboys I ever heard of.

Lew Miner was one of them—the world champion bulldogger and saddle-bronc rider in 1912 and again in 1917. He got his start right there at Calgary. Now he was working as one of the foremen at the Baker ranch. He was coming on the drive. So was Clark Lund, who was the best man with a rope I had ever seen. He got some publicity at the Calgary Stampede too. Now he worked at the Kirkaldy ranch. He was tall and lean, and so shy it was almost painful for him to say hello. Everybody liked him. He was always gentle and pretty unassuming until he stepped onto his bay mare, Maude, with a four-strand rawhide lariat in his hand. Then he became an artist. He could make a lariat do things I thought were impossible. Once, just to see how good he really was, they put him against the clock at the fall roundup. They wanted to see how fast he could rope a new calf, drag it to the branding fire, and go back for the next one. He roped seventeen of them in sixteen minutes and never missed a loop.

The last couple of days of the fall roundup, as usual, a bunch of us younger guys had been talking about going to the rodeo. Jay Knight thought he could get his dad's Ford pickup truck to make the trip. With the truck we could be there in about four hours. I asked Jacob if I could go, and of course he said no. I was needed to finish getting ready for winter at the ranch. Besides, school would be starting soon.

That made me so mad I went half a day without speaking to anybody. There wasn't a reason in the world I couldn't go to Calgary to hoorah and blow off steam with the guys. I'd only miss one day's work. I could make it up. Besides, there wasn't a thing at the ranch that was in all that big a hurry anyway.

Things were finished by midmorning on the last day, so Jay got his dad's truck. Five or six of the guys piled in and drove over to get me. It didn't take a second for me to tell them I'd go. I didn't tell Jacob or anybody. I left my horse with a friend who promised to hold it in a corral until morning, and then I was in the back of the pickup with the rest of them.

We got to Calgary around three o'clock that afternoon. There was a pretty good crowd gathering. We were all looking forward to having a real good time. I was watching the rodeo and enjoying life when some of the men from around Raymond got to kidding me about riding in the saddle-bronc competition. I was fourteen years old, and they figured it would be pretty novel to enter a kid just to see what would happen. They threw quarters into a hat until the two-dollar entry fee was raised, then signed me up. When my name was called, four men hustled me to the chute and lowered me onto a big, ugly, hammerheaded blue roan gelding that was intent on eating me alive. I wasn't about to show anyone that I was scared white, so I grinned, grabbed the hackamore rope in my left hand, jerked my hat down to my ears, and yelled, "Turn him out!" They threw open the chute gate and the roan opened the ball.

The big blue horse bucked out in a pretty straight line, letting me catch his rhythm real quick. I hit him with my spurs pretty good—first in the shoulders ahead of the cinch, then high in the flanks behind it, raking him with every jump. I held my right hand clear above my head. Nobody was going to say I had reached

17

for the saddlehorn to pull leather. No way. If I was going to get killed, I was going to die doing it right.

We were being timed by a man with a hand watch. I think he forgot to look at it. I think all he was seeing was a fourteen-year-old kid kicking the daylights out of a fourteen-hundred-pound blue roan. He was waving his hat, shouting something like, "Would you look at that crazy kid!"

I know I was up on that roan for about an hour and a half, waiting for that timekeeper to yell time. There was nothing to do but keep as good a seat as I could. I wasn't really in much of a position to mosey over to the timekeeper and suggest he might have forgotten to look at that cussed watch.

Just when I thought it was all over, he finally yelled time. The roan came back down from about two miles in the sky, the landing jarring every bone in my body. I was certain even my grandfather felt that one. I leaned back, trying to hold my spine in line with his to keep my balance. He hit the ground suddenly, only long enough to start right back up. As he went up, he unexpectedly twisted to his right. I lost my balance to my left, and I could almost feel the world coming up to collide with me. The only thing that saved my ride was that the roan twisted back to his left, right back under me so I could catch my balance when he came down again. Then I heard them holler "Time!" The pickup rider came in at my right side and jammed his running horse against the roan. I grabbed the rider around the middle and slid off the roan to the ground. As soon as my feet were down, the pickup man spun his horse and looked at me, grinning. He said something about it being "some kind of ride"—I couldn't hear it all—and I nodded my head as I trotted back to the chute.

One older rider made a better ride that day, so I won second money among the daytime contestants. Fifty dollars. As soon as I got the money, I knew where six dollars of it was going. I had seen a pair of silver-plated, hand-worked spurs during rodeo time for the last two years and wished I had the six dollars to buy them. When I got the money, I went right down to the dry-goods store to see if they still happened to be there. They were. In a minute I had the spurs on and they had my six dollars. Man, did I think I was something when I swaggered back down to the rodeo grounds. I was sure that everybody noticed those spurs and knew I'd earned them by riding a bronc to second-place money.

The rest of the guys wanted to have a little fun before we headed back. I didn't like it, but they went on down the street to the saloon to get a bottle of whisky and do a little drinking. Nothing serious; they meant no harm. I didn't drink with them, but some of them were feeling pretty good by the time it got dark.

About midnight we got back into the pickup truck and started for home. The drink had settled into some of the guys, and they were singing and being pretty loud. Occasionally one of them got sick, so we had to stop while they got out. At first I thought it was funny, but then I got disgusted, watching them bend over and retch. They traded off driving, depending on which one of them could come closest to holding the truck on the two ruts we called a road. We made a few detours out into the sagebrush, getting hung up on big clumps of brush and in badger holes a couple of times. It took some time to get the truck pushed loose when that happened, so it was nearly daybreak when we got back to Raymond.

I knew I was going to catch it from Jacob. I put my old steel spurs back on, burying the new ones in my saddlebags. I spent the ride home trying to figure out how I would handle it. I should have saved myself the worry; I couldn't get a word in edgewise.

Jacob unloaded on me. Man, I thought he was going to die right on the spot. He said the crowd I was with would lead me straight into my own ruination. He said as far as he could tell I was wild and impractical, bent on watching rodeos, avoiding work, and dreaming about the city. It was the usual lecture, only this time he added something about a wet-behind-the-ears kid of fourteen who seemed bent on getting lost on the top of Fool's Hill. According to him, there wasn't *nothing* worse than being hung on Fool's Hill and not knowing it. I hadn't even heard of Fool's Hill, but from the way he was ripping into me, I didn't have any desire for an explanation.

I got so sick of hearing it that I turned and walked away. That made Jacob all the madder. It wasn't until a day or two later that he heard somewhere that I took second money in Calgary and bought those fancy spurs for six dollars. This time he was so mad he got red in the face. I wasn't only hung on top of Fool's Hill, I was the undisputed all-time *king* of Fool's Hill. He couldn't see even a glimmer of a chance it would ever be otherwise.

I wasn't going to give him the satisfaction of asking him just what this Fool's Hill preachment was all about, and I wasn't going to make any excuses or explanations about what I had done, no matter what. I figured he'd wind down and ask about the rest of the fifty dollars, but he didn't. If he had, I was just going to tell him I'd put it away where I wanted it without telling him where it was. I had it in an old Prince Albert tobacco can under the straw mattress on my bed.

Since then I hadn't said much of anything to Jacob. What was the use? All I ever got was cussed.

I guess if the truth were known, the thing I couldn't forgive him for was the Christmas when I was eleven. Mother had saved some money, and the day before Christmas she sent Jacob to Raymond with it to get some presents for us kids. He didn't get home when we expected, and as darkness came we got pretty worried. He finally got home long after supper. The way he was walking, I knew he had been drinking, pretty bad. Mother took him straight on into the bedroom, so we didn't get to see him that night. All he brought us for Christmas was a new tin cup. Mother never told us, but I knew he had used all the Christmas money for drink. It wasn't much money to begin with, but it was all we had. I just couldn't forget the look in mother's eyes as she spent half the night doing what she could so us kids could have something on Christmas morning. For just a day or two, I hated Jacob. I wasn't going to pay him much respect until he apologized and made it right with mother and the rest of us. No matter what.

All these thoughts were hanging in my mind when I sat down for breakfast the morning I left. Mother put a plate of fried potatoes, eggs, and beef on the table for me. Jacob came into the kitchen and sat down. Mother let Elmer sleep, because he was just about down again after six days on the roundup.

I finished eating, bundled up in my scarf and coats, and pulled my hat onto my head. There wasn't a lot of emotion between us. I was leaving to do a job—a tough job—that had to be done; but that was nothing new. The whole family had been doing that ever since Jacob had built the house more than thirty years ago.

Mother said be careful, and Jacob said watch and listen to Char-

lie and Lew Miner. I told them to tell Elmer I'd bring him something from Sweetgrass. Then I went to the shed to saddle up and
load my gear.

When I finished, I stepped onto the gray and balanced the old
Springfield rifle crossways on my upper legs. The lead rope to the
sorrel was looped around my saddlehorn. I raised one hand in
good-bye as Mother and Jacob stood framed in the shaft of light
in the doorway. Then I turned the gray eastward, lightly tapping
spur to his side.

I stopped and turned only that once, to look back at the old,
unpainted, frame house where I had been born, the only home I
knew. Now, with the house out of sight behind me, I had only
trouble and turmoil inside. I got all mixed up in my head when
I remembered laughing at Elmer over the incident with the horse
and bucket and berries. I didn't mean any harm by laughing at
him. It was just a lot funnier to be me watching than to be him
getting bucked off. Couldn't he see that? I didn't need a lecture
from him. I just needed him to see the humor in it. Why couldn't
he? The worst part of my mixed-up feelings came from trying to
figure him walking out to hand me his lariat. I almost wished he
hadn't done it, in a way.

And Jacob. Last summer when he got to lecturing me just about
every day and then jumped all over me for going to the rodeo, I
had decided I wouldn't talk to him much more until he started
showing some sign of giving me a little credit. Why wasn't he
willing to look at his own weaknesses and correct them? Why
couldn't he show me a little confidence? A little trust?

Struggling to clear my mind, I finally realized that the biggest
problem was that Jacob and Elmer just didn't understand. The
trouble between me and them was mostly because they were
pretty unfair and opinionated and unable to see things from my
point of view. Maybe they'd have some time to think it over and
change a little while I was gone. I sure hoped they'd work on it.

The horizon to the east was beginning to show the separation
of the sky and the earth. I saw a few lights winking on in Raymond and realized I had covered five miles, lost in my thoughts.

From this point on I didn't have time to worry about Elmer and
Jacob. I had to give my job as a drover the best that was in me.
And I was going to show father he was wrong about me.

Chapter Three

I approached town as rose-colored
streaks began to show in the deep purple of the few scattered
clouds to the east. I turned the gray a little south, skirting the
dark, unpainted houses and buildings, riding directly to the herd.
Within minutes I had given the Springfield rifle and the twenty
bullets to Charlie MacDonald, turned the sorrel mare in with the
other horses, and taken my assignment for the day from Charlie.
A little while later, when it looked like all the others were there,
Charlie sent out word for us all to gather by the fire. On David
Baker's signal, Charlie stepped out to face us.

"I've been asked to do what speakin' is necessary. The ranchers
providin' the riders fer the gather of this herd have spent consid-
erable time reachin' some conclusions. The way it shapes up, it
looks like we either cut the number of cattle on the range by over
half or we lose 'em all by spring, along with the range grass fer
at least the next five years. It will break us all. Anyone see that
different than I said it?"

Everybody looked around, but no one spoke to the contrary.

"I've been asked to be trail boss for a cattle drive to Sweetgrass,
where we'll load the heifers and steers onto cattle cars fer Chicago. I'll sell 'em there fer the best price I can get. The way we
estimate it right now, we have to fetch about eighteen dollars a
head fer the twenty-eight hundred we figure to cut out. That'll

give us enough cash money to see most of us through, with some left over to restock in the next year or two. Is there any disagreement?"

Again no one spoke.

"I've asked Lew Miner to be my number-two man. We're takin' eight more men fer crew. They'll be paid usual wages out of the money we get fer the cattle. I'll keep a daily log as usual, and I'll be accountable to all of ye fer what finally happens, except fer the price. I can't be responsible fer that. The best quotations we can get over the telegraph at Calgary is that range stock in poor condition is bringin' anywhere from fifteen dollars to nineteen dollars a head right now, this bein' the off season. Good and prime beef is bringin' from nineteen to twenty-four. Today when we make the sort, we'll make a voucher fer every ranch owner, showin' the number of cattle he has in the herd accordin' to his brand. When I get back, the money after expenses and wages will be divided among the owners accordin' to their voucher, share and share alike. That way each one winds up payin' his share of the wages and standin' his share of the losses we're bound to have on the trail. Anyone disagree with that?"

All heads shook no, because it was the fairest way to handle it.

"We got a long day ahead of us, so I don't see much sense in sayin' more unless one of you do."

He waited, but no one spoke. Charlie started to turn away but then stopped and faced us again.

"I guess I should also say that no one ever heard of trail drivin' twenty-eight hundred cattle for a week in the middle of January, from where we are to where we're goin'. I have some notion of the risks. I know where we're all goin' to be if somethin' goes wrong. I can only promise ye I'll do what I can to finish this job, and I know the job ain't done until we got the money back here in the bank. With the Good Lord willin', we'll make it. I guess that's all."

He turned as a little buzz of talking started. Then everybody went to their horses and we settled into our work.

All day, twenty of us held the big herd bunched while men mounted on cutting horses patiently located and cut out the steers and heifers for the drive south. A little after noon I took my turn at the chuckwagon, eating the steaming stew and hardtack, washing it down with coffee so hot it burned your mouth. I said my thanks to the cook before I went to the horses to exchange the gray for the sorrel mare. A minute later I was back with the herd, helping hold them in a bunch while the cutting continued.

We finished late in the afternoon. The big herd stood divided into two smaller ones. The tally showed that 2,831 head of steers and heifers had been cut into a separate herd, ready for the drive. The brood cows and range bulls in the other herd would be held and moved north a couple of miles, then turned back on the range after we left in the morning.

The tough decisions were behind us, the preparation finished. Our assignments and our minds were clear. Excitement was in the air so strong you could cut it with a knife.

The cook banged on the big black iron triangle that called us to supper, and the crew turned their horses toward the fire by the chuckwagon to take their rotation for the victuals. Vapor clouds trailed behind their heads and from the nostrils of their horses.

The nine of us who had been picked to move the herd to Sweetgrass gathered around Charlie. "I've talked to each of ye, and ye know my rules fer the drive," he said. "I ain't pretendin' I know what it's goin' to be like makin' a drive like this in this weather, but if we'll just keep our wits about us, we'll make it. I just want to remind ye, half the southern end of the Province of Alberta is goin' broke if we don't win this gamble. So we're goin' to win."

He pulled a map from inside his coat, unfolded it, and laid it on the ground. We all hunkered down, following his finger as he traced the route.

The little town of Raymond is on the east slope of the Continental Divide. Just north of it is Lethbridge, and farther up, Calgary; just south, Magrath. West were the Rocky Mountains, the tops of which formed the Divide. East, north, and south was the continental watershed, a great slope of grass-covered rolling prairie that ran for hundreds of miles. All rivers flowed eastward on our side of the Divide.

By angling south and east, we were going to cross the McIntyre Lease, as we called it, which was just a great tract of open ground leased for running cattle. We would continue across the homestead lands, which were wide open prairie except for a homesteader's cabin once in a great while. We would see none of them. About thirty or so miles farther south, just past the old Fort Benton trail, running pretty well east and west, was the Milk River. The Milk River Ridge rose from the prairie floor on this side of the river. It wasn't very high; it served more as a landmark than a barrier, but we had to cross it. Past the ridge and the river, sixty-eight miles south and east of us, was the tiny town of Sweetgrass. Barely on the Montana side of the international boundary, Sweetgrass had a railroad spur of the Great Northern Railway that traveled south and connected to the main line at Cut Bank. From there the main line went east along the Milk River and then the Missouri River, across Montana and North Dakota, and angled southeast through Minnesota and Wisconsin to Chicago, Illinois.

Our job was to deliver the cattle to Sweetgrass. Figuring we could move that many cattle about ten miles a day, we expected to have them there about the seventh day after we started the drive.

Charlie had arranged for some of the ranchers to drop loads of grass hay from their ranches at designated places on the route so we would have enough feed for the cattle for the first few days. They would get enough moisture as long as the snow held on the ground. We would have to depend on the land for feed and water after the fifth night.

Charlie carefully traced the route with his finger, pointing out all the landmarks—old watering holes and sinks, some points of high ground, the Milk River Ridge, and a few others. He looked at us and asked for questions. There were none. We were ready, eager.

We had been picked because we were mostly single men without family responsibilities at home on the ranches. Only two of us were married. One was Lew Miner, and the other was a German fellow named Fritz Hoffman. Charlie had lost his wife and two children years ago when smallpox swept through the Province, leaving more than a third of the people in the Indian nations dead and a lot of the settlers along with them. The faces of many of those who survived still showed the deep scarring from the pox. For reasons I wouldn't learn about until later, Charlie had never remarried to start another family. Instead, he buried himself in the work at the Baker ranch. As the years passed, he rose to the position of ranch manager. Crusty and tough and fair, he spoke little, but when he did, people listened. Even David Baker listened.

Lew's wife, Kitty, was about as good with stock as Lew was. Whatever needed to be done while he was gone, she could do. I was glad Clark Lund was going, too. I knew three of the remaining men well enough to say hello to them, but the others were pretty well strangers to me.

Charlie told me I was to drive the chuckwagon the first half day, until we got close to the Kirkaldy ranch headquarters. The Kirkaldy riders would meet us there to lend us their Chinese cook for the trip. Clark Lund said the cook was an honest-to-goodness Chinaman from China, pigtail and all, who couldn't speak much English, but he was a good cook. Call him Cookie, Clark warned us. Don't call him "Hey you," or "chink," or anything else. Just Cookie. Clark said he saw the little man grab a cleaver one day and chase a loudmouth out of the ranch cookshack. The man had made some sort of a wisecrack about the braided pigtail and "the little chink."

We all smiled. In near-record cold, with more than a week of almost no sleep ahead of us and the daily possibility of severe problems, the prospect of having good, solid, hot food three times a day seemed like a gift from Providence. If this blessing came from a Chinaman with a pigtail who had to be called Cookie, that was okay with us. For three hot square meals a day we'd have called him King George the Third.

While I ate supper I studied the ones on the crew that I didn't know too well. Afterward I stood around the big fire for a little while, quiet, listening to everything the others were saying before I rolled out my bedroll.

That night I slept wrapped in the three blankets and the heavy canvas tarp, with only my boots and my hat off. I rolled the boots into the tarp to keep them free of the heavy frost that would cover us before morning. For the next eight days, the rock-hard ground would be my bed and the heavy frost would be my morning companion.

I will never forget the excitement I felt as I rolled out of my blankets in the early gray dawn the following morning. As men born to cattle and the land do, I first put on my hat, then fumbled in the bedroll for my high-heeled boots with the old steel spurs still in place. I loosened the spur straps so I could get my feet to make the turn into the bottoms of the boots, and tightened the straps again before I stood up. I put my bedroll in the chuckwagon, ready to start. I didn't expect the shiver of anticipation that ran through me as I looked out at the herd.

After a breakfast of hot oatmeal, sausage, and coffee, I harnessed the chuckwagon's two horses, checking the singletrees and tugs, and climbed into the driver's seat.

I almost felt like I was in a dream. Sitting there wrapped to my eyes in the scarf and coat, reins in my hands, I watched as Charlie gave the orders. John Sweet, twenty-one years old, was assigned as the scout. He wore a chin string on his hat and had a sort of easygoing, carefree, devil-may-care attitude. For all-around savvy with horses and cows, Sweet was tops. Rumor had it he was one-quarter Crow Indian, but none of us was sure of it, nor did we care. He stood about six feet tall, weighed about 180 pounds, and was strong in the arms and shoulders. His black hair accented his dark eyes and swarthy skin. Sweet didn't have any family anyone knew about. He had just sort of been around since any of us could remember, on his own. He had a reputation that was a puzzle. Some called him a renegade while some called him a saint. Some feared him, others saw him as a close friend. He had been in a few fights and brawls over the years, and some said the change from the easygoing man we knew to a brutal, tough brawler came fast. When it happened, he was hard to beat. Just being around him for this short time I sensed there was some thunder and lightning in him. If it ever got out, I could believe someone might do some suffering.

That morning when Charlie nodded to him, Sweet grinned with that reckless, carefree air of his, spun his horse, and loped out strong ahead of the herd. He was watching the ground, the water, the grass for feed, and looking for bedground for the night. It was Sweet's job to be sure the mapped route was clear and passable. If it wasn't, he had to find one that was.

Then Lew Miner touched spur to his horse and loped out to the south end of the herd to ride point. Two men, Joseph Swensen and Tommy Bascom, trotted their horses to the east side of the herd, taking their positions as flankers. Two good, steady men.

Douglas Owens and Clark Lund moved out and spaced themselves as flankers on the west side. Doug Owens was a quiet, reliable man. Clark Lund fit in and did his job no matter where he was.

Bill Ackersley and Fritz Hoffman dropped in behind the herd of horses, ready to move them out with the cattle when Charlie signaled. Bill could hold his place as a drover too. Fritz was a quiet man, good with livestock. He was shy and seemed to have something on his mind most of the time. I knew his wife had just birthed a new baby boy last spring, so I figured he was a little worried about leaving her with the new baby and their three-year-old daughter for this long in the dead of winter.

Our assignments would change from time to time except for Sweet and Lew. Sweet was our scout, Lew our point man for the drive.

Charlie MacDonald chose to ride drag. When all the men had reached their positions and turned to watch Charlie, he waved his hat in the air and whistled. As though by magic, it all came alive.

The flankers moved in, yelling to get the cattle off the bedground. The last flanker on either side rode in among the cattle a short distance, talking, yelling, swinging the loose ends of their lariats to get the cattle started south. Soon the sea of horns and hides started to move—slowly at first, then at an even walk, with Lew leading them.

Caught up in the power and the wonder of it, I sat in a sort of trance for several minutes. I knew I was watching one of the last cattle drives, at least of that size, that our part of the country would ever see. I can still feel the awe and the thrill that went through me that frosty morning, watching those nine men start twenty-eight hundred cattle south. The prairie was wide open. There wasn't a fence between us and Sweetgrass. There wasn't a mountain or a tree to break the plainness, the silent, lonely emptiness, of the rolling, brush-covered land—nothing between us and the place where land met sky miles to the south.

At noon a buckboard from the Kirkaldy ranch caught up, carrying the cook. He was wrapped in so many coats and topped off by such a funny-looking knitted wool hat that we couldn't tell whether he was Chinese or an Eskimo. Without a word he took over the chuckwagon from me, and in short order the noon meal was steaming and ready. Clark had been right. He might be Chinese, but he sure cooked Canadian.

I wolfed down my plate of beef and gravy and biscuits and gulped down hot coffee. Then I went to the herd of shaggy, winter-haired horses to drop my loop over the gray. Within minutes I was mounted. Charlie had told me to drop in as drag rider opposite him, behind the east flankers, and keep my eyes open for herd-quitters and strays. I didn't need to be told. I knew how to ride drag. I touched a gloved finger to my hat brim to signal that I was heading to my assignment, then loped out beside the east side of the herd.

I don't think words exist to describe the feeling that rises in a man's soul when he is well mounted and working cattle. He is a king presiding over his kingdom. Life is simple and understandable, clean and right.

In gathering dusk we made it to the first feed drop and bedded the cattle for the night. We had covered just more than ten miles that first day. After the warmth of supper had settled in, I went to my blankets bone weary and slept a deep, dreamless sleep. I know I slept smiling.

Chapter Four

At dawn the second day, as we quit our blankets and made our bedrolls, we all had an uneasy feeling. There was something different in the air. No one mentioned it, but we were all a little quieter. We finished the hot meal Cookie had waiting, then moved out to our assignments, feeling just a little unsettled.

Cattle act a lot like people on a cattle drive. Pretty soon the leaders show up leading, and the followers fall in behind them. A kind of natural marching order starts to appear. Once that is established, things move along pretty good.

After we pushed the cattle off the bedground, they milled around into a sort of formation, with the leaders out front. We continued southward, settling them into the routine they were beginning to understand. By midmorning we were spending a lot less time trying to hold them bunched and they were moving with less and less direction from us. They were becoming an organization, a unit. We felt good; the uneasiness was almost forgotten.

But after our noon meal that feeling came over us again of something being out of place. It suddenly dawned on us what was wrong. The air was dead. Nothing was moving. It felt like a hush had settled in. For the first time we noticed that the cattle's heads were up, their ears pointing. Our horses had their heads up too, and they were skittish. We also realized that the temperature had risen, maybe fifteen degrees. It was still a long way below freezing, but we could feel it was warmer.

Then I knew. We had been so absorbed in getting the cattle off to a good start we hadn't been paying attention to the weather. I glanced to the east and even as I did, the first stirring of a breeze passed over us.

A Canadian blizzard was moving in.

We stepped onto our nervous horses and trotted to our assigned positions, glancing to the east. Winter storms usually moved into the prairie from the west, and they were bad enough. The ones from the east were usually the worst. If this one got bad, the drive could be over before it got started—over, and maybe some of us gone right along with the cattle.

By two o'clock in the afternoon we could see great low clouds the color of bullet lead moving our way. By four o'clock they scudded over us, filled with snow, and locked us into a dark, gray world. All talk stopped, but we kept the cattle moving on the route Charlie had showed us. Every eye was watching as we tried to judge how bad it would be.

The cattle got too quiet. Too many of their heads were up and moving from side to side. Their fear of a real blizzard was as bad as ours. Somehow, animals usually seem to know more than men about what mother nature's doing. I was riding the sorrel and she was fighting the bit just a little, ears twitching, her movements jerky.

We didn't know how big this one was; we didn't know if we were in the center of it or out on one of the edges. All we were sure of was that we had 2,831 head of range cattle that were getting real nervous. By now we were all frightened. The expression on Charlie's face hadn't changed, but there was fear in his eyes.

But we had to bury our fears and keep moving, hoping Sweet, out riding scout, could find bedground where we could hold them through the night. On this flat prairie that seemed impossible. You see, in a killer blizzard cattle will turn their rumps to the wind and drift with it until the storm dies. If this storm turned out to be a real howler and these cattle drifted with it on this flat land, the ten of us wouldn't stand a chance of holding them bunched. The herd could scatter for thirty miles or more over this fenceless prairie in the next day or two, and we couldn't do a thing about it. Deep snow could lock them into drifts that would hold them until they starved. We wouldn't find them all until next spring, and then we would only find the bones and hides. If it got bad enough we would be locked into drifts right along with them. If we got drifted in, and then the temperatures dropped twenty degrees and held, it would be all over for a lot of cattle and horses. Maybe for some of us, too.

Charlie's eyes moved constantly as he searched the horizon to the south, straining to pick up the silhouette of John Sweet. Sweet's chances of finding any sort of natural break on this flat prairie where we could hold the cattle against a blizzard were darned slim. It would almost be a miracle if he did.

The wind was rising. We pulled our coats tighter and our hats low, hunching ourselves against it. As the first few snowflakes slanted at us, we heard a faint yell above the wind. Instantly every head jerked toward the south, searching. There was Sweet, a black silhouette on the horizon. He waved his hat until he knew we saw him. Then he made a long, slow arc with his arm that ended with him pointing south and a little east. To us he looked like the angel Gabriel.

He was pointing a direction for us. We could only trust him and keep the cattle moving. We spurred our horses into the herd, raising them to a walk, then a trot, following the ramrod-straight back of Lew Miner. We almost feared to hope that Sweet had found bedground.

In the fast-fading light, Lew Miner raised his hand, pointing slightly east, to his left, before he disappeared over the rise where we had seen Sweet. The cattle followed, looking like a moving, flowing river. The flankers crowded them, yelling, holding them bunched against the gathering wind and snow. Charlie and I kept our horses moving, jamming the drags back into the rear of the herd.

Sweet hadn't come back to help move the cattle onto the bedground, wherever it was. As Charlie and I crested the little rise where we had last seen Lew, we saw the reason.

In the last light of day we could see where a long-forgotten, tremendous cloudburst had left its mark. The water had carved a great gash in the prairie floor in its headlong rush to some unknown tributary farther down the continental slope. Left behind was a bank perhaps twelve feet high in a gentle easterly curve from north to south. It made a sort of U-shaped natural corral that opened only to the west, which is exactly the direction we were coming from.

If the cattle reached the bank and then started south, they might want to turn back to the west to drift with the storm back onto the prairie. To stop any cattle that took that notion, Sweet had taken up a position at the far southern side of the U shape. Lew had ridden over to help him, the two of them closing the only outlet.

We pushed the cattle right up against the bank and strung ourselves out in a line across the open side of the corral nature had provided. With an axe and our lariats we cut brush and dragged it into huge piles spaced at regular intervals. We sprinkled the brush with coal oil from the chuckwagon so it would burn. Despite the rising wind and the thick, wet snow, we got the fires started.

We were still more than three miles short of the next feed drop, but none of us even thought about it. If we didn't hold the cattle, the feed didn't matter. We'd have to let them get what they could as they moved past it tomorrow or the next day.

The gray gloom of fading light soon yielded to a blackness broken only by the huge fires burning at intervals along the mouth of the corral. While half of us rode the fire line, watching for drifters and holding the cattle against the bank, the other half fed the fires. Then we traded jobs. Cookie made hot food and coffee, and we took brief turns at the chuckwagon, handing back our empty tin plates with thanks before moving back to the line.

While we worked, Sweet told Charlie he figured we were on the very south edge of the storm. When it came rolling in, he had been three, four miles ahead of the herd and could see the storm northeast of us. But to the south he had seen a slight sliver of blue sky before he turned back to signal us. If that was the southern edge of the storm like he figured, it would blow itself out sometime tomorrow as it moved northward. We could only hope he was right.

Cattle won't move against a fire. If we could keep them going and keep all of us moving between them, we stood a chance of holding the cattle bunched, despite their tendency to drift with the wind. We also figured the twelve-foot bank on the east gave them a sort of wind break. Maybe they would hold right there, letting the wind blow over them. With all these "ifs" and "maybes," there wasn't much we could do but get ready for a long, cold night sitting in wet saddles on horses wet with the clinging snow, battling to hold the herd.

By midnight we dared to begin believing we could hold them until dawn. Despite the snow and the wind we still had the fires going, and we could see the near edge of the herd. The cattle were bawling and milling, their wide eyes reflecting the firelight, showing their fear of the storm's power.

But at one o'clock in the morning the temperature dropped and the wind picked up. The snow was coming in small, stinging, icy flakes, slanting, forcing us to squint to see the eyes and rumps and horns of the closest cattle as we steadily rode the fire line. We were in the teeth of a killer Canadian blizzard. Without the fires we wouldn't have been able to see our hands in front of our faces.

By three o'clock, we knew we were going to lose the fires. The wet brush began to smolder in the howling wind; then the fires were gone. The wind snatched our shouted words, instantly smothering them. If the cattle had started to run we wouldn't have been able to hear it.

We spread out in a line west of the herd and faced the storm, moving constantly, yelling as hard as we could to try to seal off the opening. We knew a few were getting past us, because we could feel them bumping into our horses. The only thing we could do was keep moving and keep shouting.

Finally the gray of daybreak filtered slowly across the prairie. By eight o'clock the wind was slowing just a little, the snow thinning. At last we could make out the herd standing between us and the bank to the east. We looked like ghosts, horses and riders plastered white with the sticky snow that had hardened when the temperature dropped earlier.

Sweet had ridden to the top of the bank and was facing us, looking down on the snow-covered herd, calculating how much of it was left. Lew was to the south making his tally, and Charlie was counting to the north. Sweet came loping off the bank toward Lew, who fell in beside him. They approached Charlie, their horses' feet throwing snow behind them, vapor trailing from their horses' muzzles.

In the muffled silence of the newly fallen snow, we listened breathlessly as they compared their tallies, and heard them say that not quite two hundred had gotten past us in the night.

We couldn't believe it. Somehow we had held most of them.

Chapter Five

While we changed our jaded horses for fresh ones, Cookie turned out some steaming hot coffee and fried bread. We didn't have time for a full breakfast. With molasses-covered bread and tin mugs of hot coffee in our hands, we listened to Charlie's orders.

We were to go out in teams—Lew Miner and me to the north, Clark Lund and Douglas Owens south. Each team would cut a wide circle four or five miles to the west, then move back together, spacing ourselves apart as we approached the herd. We were to move as fast as we could in the snow, bringing back all the strays we could find. Sweet would go southeast to find out how far south the storm had hit and look for a route through the snow.

We finished our grub and mounted the fresh horses, and without a word the five of us moved out.

Lew and I raised our horses to a trot, moving north and west with the wind, making good time. The snow stood about a foot deep on the wind-swept flat and several feet deep in the drifts. An hour out we made our move back to the south toward where we expected to find Clark and Doug. We hadn't crossed a single set of cattle tracks in the five miles we'd covered, so we believed the cattle had drifted due west from the herd. We hoped they were between us and the other two riders. We waited a few minutes, watching for Clark and Doug, aware that the wind was dying and the snow was thinning rapidly.

Then suddenly we could see the other two mounted men, moving black dots in a world of white. We shouted and waved, turning our heads a little to listen. They returned the shouts. Lew and I spaced ourselves with them. In a line, we started back toward the east.

We found the drifters by twos and threes in some places, eights and tens in others, and collected them into the beginnings of a small herd. Wearily they turned their wet, snow-matted heads to the east, moving ahead of us as we hollered and talked to them. We rode back and forth, keeping them bunched, gathering others as we moved.

By noon we could see the main herd. Charlie came out to meet us, quartering off to one side so he wouldn't break the flow of the cattle, which were now moving steadily due east.

He reined in and sat still as he started a count while they passed him. You don't count moving cattle by ones. You count them in clumps—three or four, or even six or seven at a time. Your eye just has to know at one glance how many are in a clump, and you have to mentally add that many to the running total you keep in your mind. *Never* interrupt a man in the middle of a running count. If he loses his concentration he has to start over. As we came on in, the crew opened a corridor so our little bunch could melt right back into the main herd up against the bank.

We gathered back at the chuckwagon, waiting for Charlie to tell us how many we had.

"I counted 188 head."

I looked at Lew, unable to hold back a little grin. Of the two hundred head we guessed had drifted, we had brought back all but twelve. We wouldn't know the actual losses for sure until we counted them onto the cattle cars at Sweetgrass—but for now, coming through that howler with all but twelve head was more than we really had a right to expect. It was close to a miracle. None of us were counting the losses by the head, we were counting them by the dollar. One animal meant about fifteen dollars. Twelve of them meant $180. Right now, $180 would look like a king's ransom to some of the small ranchers back home.

Charlie got out his little pencil stub and notebook to make the entries in the daily log, recording the date and the losses. That log would be the basis for the accounting of the 2,831 cattle entrusted to his care. Typical of Charlie, it would be as complete as possible.

It was now one o'clock in the afternoon. The snow had stopped and the wind had almost totally died. The clouds moved north and west, and soon little breaks began to show in the solid gray that had hovered over us all morning. Cookie banged on the triangle and we started our rotation for the noon meal—hot sliced beef on biscuits, thick gravy on potatoes and carrots, all of it washed down with hot coffee. Food had never tasted better.

We couldn't move the cattle until Sweet returned with a report, so we just held them in a bunch against the bank and waited. As the afternoon wore on, little else was necessary except staying mounted and moving back and forth across the mouth of the corral. After their wild night fighting the roaring wind and the stinging ice and snow, the cattle were content to stay bunched.

By three that afternoon clear breaks were showing in the clouds. The storm was continuing its sweep, leaving us behind. Most of us had been in the saddle for thirty-two straight hours. Fourteen of those hours had been in darkness as we endured the battering wind and ice and snow.

I was at the north end of the line, keeping the gray moving at a walk, just beginning to feel the letdown after the crisis. A sense of weariness was spreading through me. I felt thankful for the chance to just sit on the gray and let him walk. With the warm food inside me and the quiet, white world around me, I felt a sense of well-being, thinking about what we had done. The steady rhythm of the walking of the gray smoothed out, and my thoughts drifted. I thought of mother, hoping she wouldn't worry about me when the blizzard hit our home range. As my mind wandered it seemed like the gray stopped and the world became still and quiet and warm. I thought I could even hear mother calling my name.

"Lad, are you all right?"

The thick Scottish accent jolted me back to the world. I had fallen asleep in the saddle, and when the gray realized it he had stopped. Charlie had noticed me sitting the patient horse, my head tipped forward, not moving, and he had loped up to check on me.

Facing Charlie I felt ashamed and embarrassed. "Yeah, Mr.

MacDonald, I'm all right. I guess I dozed off. Mr. MacDonald, I don't know how . . . I'm sorry. It won't happen again."

I knew I had done one of the few things you can't do on a cattle drive. There are times when the whole crew depends on you, and one of those times is when you're assigned to hold cattle bunched. If one man lets down, the rest of the crew can pay a terrible price. Each man was entitled to *know* he could trust the others, and I had broken the code. A trailhand asleep on the job is held in pretty low regard by the others.

"It's all right, lad. Can ye stay awake until supper?"

"Yes, sir. I won't let it happen again. Not ever. I hope you'll . . ."

He cut me off. "No harm done, lad. But keep a sharp eye. As I came up on ye I saw a great gray wolf about three, four hundred yards due north of ye. After a blizzard like last night they'll be hangin' off a little distance, waitin' to pull down a stray or one that is too far gone to fight back. It's important I know if ye see one. Keep a sharp eye." He turned his horse back toward the herd.

I touched spur to the gray and reined him back to the north. I don't know how long I had been asleep. I felt sick inside, angry at myself. I hit my fist against the saddlehorn in disgust, cursing myself.

From that moment until dark I covered my assigned territory head up, watching everything. The cattle were quiet and still, and there was no wolf.

At dusk Cookie banged the triangle. I came to the chuckwagon on my rotation for supper not knowing whether anyone knew I had fallen asleep or what kind of reception I would get. I felt like keeping quiet. No one made a comment about it or even seemed to know.

I had just gotten my tin plate of hot fried beef strips and potatoes and carrots when Charlie turned, looking to the south. I don't know how he knew Sweet was there, but a bit later the rest of us saw him too, coming in at a lope.

He laid his map out on the tailgate of the chuckwagon, and with Charlie and the rest of us on the shift gathered around intently watching and listening, he made his report.

He had been right yesterday about the location of the storm. We were on the south edge. About seven, eight miles south of us, the snow petered out. His finger slowly moving on the map, he traced a wrinkle in the prairie, due east about a mile, that pushed up to a small crest that ran south and then angled southeast. The wind had swept most of the snow from the east side and dumped it on our side. We would have to break through a mile of drifts to get over the crest, but once on the east side we could follow the crest on bare ground all the way southeast to where the snow let up. About three miles down the clear side was the feed we had intended to reach last night. The next feed drop was ten miles farther southeast, past where the snow petered out. Those last ten miles were slightly downhill. All told, it made for just more than fourteen miles with tired cattle, in one day. Sweet thought it could be done if we started before daylight and pushed hard all day.

Charlie considered, then nodded. He told Sweet he had done a good job. He was to go have a warm supper and get into his blankets until morning.

We all knew tomorrow would start in the dark of the morning and finish in the dark of the night. We would eat food from our hands as we rode, with no time out of the saddle.

I imagined for a minute telling father and Elmer all about the blizzard. How me and three others had gone out the morning after to bring back nearly every critter that had drifted during the night. That ought to impress them. But if I did, I'd have to tell about the stinging embarrassment of having dozed in the saddle while I was supposed to be holding the cattle. Maybe I could end the story before I got that far.

I pushed the thought out of my mind as I considered what the next day would bring. The trail gives little time to dream about glory or worry about mistakes.

Chapter Six

It seemed like I had just rolled up in my blankets and tarp when I felt a hand shake me. I had slept five hours.

Standing at the breakfast fire, I finished the hot oatmeal mush with hot tea and biscuits. We all stuffed half a dozen biscuits and some dried apple slices into our coat pockets, knowing our next hot meal would be under the stars that night. Five minutes later I was on the sorrel moving out to my assigned position.

With the morning star just beginning to fade, we started talking to the cattle, rousting them off their bedground, moving them west out of the mouth of the corral. Then we turned them almost completely around and started southeast through the foot-deep snow.

Within half an hour we were pushing the cattle up the incline on our side of the crest, straight into the heavy concentration of snowdrifts. Lew and the lead flankers, breaking trail for the cattle, spurred their horses into the drifts. At times we would lose sight of a horse altogether as it stepped into snow six or eight feet deep. Then up it would come, head high, blowing snow out of its nostrils and shaking it out of its mane and hide, plunging, jumping, trying to find the bottom of the drift. Breaking trail through snowdrifts can drain a horse and rider real fast.

About forty minutes later Lew rose to the top of the crest and dropped out of sight on the far side. He had made it! The flowing river of snow-matted hides and horns was widening the trail he had opened and was moving over the crest onto bare, hard, icy prairie. By eleven we were on clear ground on the southeast face of the crest, just as Sweet had described. The cattle moved under a cold, clear sky in full, frigid sunshine. About one o'clock we slowed nearly to a stop so the cattle could graze through the hay drop as they moved southeast. Two hours later we reached the southeast end of the crest. We could see the prairie ahead of us, patches of grass showing here and there. The cattle pulled it as they passed, chewing it as they walked. We kept the pressure on them, watching the westering sun as we calculated the miles we had yet to cover to find the next feed drop and bedground.

At dusk Sweet appeared on the next gentle rise, waving his hat and we knew we were close. We kept the pressure on, weary men driving weary cattle. Inside, we felt a tired glow of satisfaction. We had moved twenty-eight hundred cattle over fourteen miles in one day. And that included opening nearly a mile of drifts to get them over the crest.

We arrived at the feed drop in full darkness, and the cattle stopped among the scattered piles of hay. We could hear them chewing the grass hay, then working their cuds. Bone weary, we pointed our exhausted horses toward the cookfire, savoring the thought of warmth and supper.

The three men who had the first herd assignment, from eight o'clock until midnight, were given first helping at Cookie's hot meal. They ate like they had never seen food before. Reluctantly they put away their plates, nodded their thanks, and mounted up to take their positions.

The rest of us loaded our plates and gathered near the fire. We moved slowly, our legs and backs stiff from fifteen hours in the saddle. Wearily, with little talk, we ate the food, staring at the dancing flames of Cookie's fire.

Clark Lund and Fritz Hoffman and I were given the last shift before dawn. We were so tired it was an effort to get our bedrolls out of the chuckwagon and spread them near the fire. No one was saying much as we finished. It was then that Bill Ackersley dropped one that stopped us all for just a minute.

He had been so tired he had almost forgotten to mention the big gray wolf he'd seen about half a mile east of the herd. Charlie and I exchanged glances. It looked like Charlie's wolf had followed the herd.

Wolves usually don't come as singles. If you see one, you can almost depend on more of them being around somewhere. They work as teams. If you study them you learn they are like a family, each with an assignment. If one among them is smart and bold enough, the team sometimes moves into a bunch of cattle to start some of them running. They keep them running until the cattle either drop over or come to a stop to fight. If a cow drops over, the wolves kill it outright. If it stands to fight, they pull it down by cutting the hamstrings with their teeth so the cow can't maneuver, making the kill easy. Either way, the wolves have a feast and some rancher has one less cow.

Charlie spoke up. "It might be the one I saw yesterday, which means it's followed us lookin' for cripples or strays. This is a big herd, and the cattle are tuckered. I don't know if they'll spook if wolves come sniffin', but keep a sharp eye and ear on yer shift. If ye see cattle up and millin', or hear them bawlin' when they shouldn't be, get back here fer help. Do ye understand?"

We didn't need to be told. Cattle get real nervous when wolves get bold enough to come nipping into a herd. Tired cattle will sometimes stand and fight, but no one can ever predict what it will take to start them running, day or night. Nothing I know of strikes fear into the hearts of a trail crew worse than the terror of a night stampede.

Charlie rode out to tell the other three about the wolf. I started working on how this story could best be used to let father and Elmer know I'd been part of another important event.

A little later we went to our blankets with a rising sense of concern. Would these exhausted cattle run if old Lobo came prowling?

Chapter Seven

Fifteen minutes before four o'clock, Clark and Fritz and I walked to the horse herd in the dark carrying our saddles, stirrups dragging on the ground, saddle blankets in our hand. I had stuffed my bridle inside my coat to try to warm the bit before I worked it into the gray's mouth. Once saddled and mounted, we silently turned our separate ways to our assigned positions.

I was replacing Doug Owens. I located him by the sound of his voice as he talked quietly to the cattle—"Huuuuuu there cattle," over and over again, to soothe them and give them a sense of security. The wolf scare had made all of us jittery, and the one thing we didn't want was to suddenly come up on the cattle without them knowing we were there. All we needed was to have about twenty surprised cattle on one side of the herd suddenly grunt and heave themselves off the bedground and start milling around, bawling. In five seconds we could have the rest of the herd up, nervous, not knowing what caused the fuss, afraid and ready to run.

As Doug passed me I asked quietly, "Everything okay?"

"Yeah, generally. About twenty minutes ago something had a few of 'em up and talking to each other up at the north end of the herd, but it seems like they settled down again."

We both stopped. "Wolf?"

That question had been riding heavy on all our shoulders all through the night. "Could have been. I doubt it. They're quiet now." As he turned toward the chuckwagon he said, "Henry, be careful."

I didn't need to be told. I moved into his position talking low and quiet, slowly moving the gray on the outer edge of the herd. I made everything seem calm, but I wasn't calm inside. I was hearing every sound, straining my eyes to see anything that moved or didn't look right.

My position was on the east side of the herd, at about the middle. My assignment was to ride south, following the edge of the herd as it curved to the west. After I had gone around about a third of the perimeter I turned around and retraced my steps to where I had started. Opposite me, Fritz Hoffman was doing the same thing, so every now and then we met at the south end of the herd. At the north end Clark Lund was doing the same, so occasionally I met him at the place we both turned around. That way each of us got to speak to the other two men to report anything that needed to be talked about.

Six o'clock came and went. To the east we could make out the horizon against the first gray of dawn. I started to sit easier, feeling the tension drain out of my back and shoulders. We had gotten through the night, and our fears about the wolves began to fade with the coming of light.

Finishing another leg of my round, I heard Clark talking low as he approached. I waited a minute to say hello. He dismounted and put his hands on his hips, leaning back to relieve the tension in his back muscles. I stepped down beside him to stretch and give the gray a minute or two without my weight on him.

"Been quiet?" Clark asked.

"Yes, nothin' movin'." We both felt relief at having gotten through the night.

Suddenly our horses heads swung up, ears pointing, eyes staring north into the dark at something neither of us could see or hear.

In the next three seconds the whole world went crazy. It happened so fast we had no time to think. The horses started dancing around and pulling at the reins. We jerked our heads north, but in the gray light we could hardly see our side of the herd. We heard a little drumming sound that swelled to a rumble, and the ground under us began to tremble.

Then Clark screamed at me, *"They're runnin'! Move, Henry!"*

The horses knew what was happening before we did. When Clark yelled they had already turned south to run with the cattle. We grabbed the saddlehorns and swung up; they were moving at a full run before we hit the saddle seats. From nowhere cattle were suddenly all around us, legs driving, jamming, heedless, mindless, seeing nothing, not knowing or caring. Eleven thousand churning hooves shook the ground, raising a thunder that drowned out every other sound.

I remember only two things about the next couple of minutes. First, I felt fear that reached clear to my bones. Second, I thought that the gray had the best chance of any horse I knew to make that desperate life-or-death run in the darkness. I had gentled him when I was ten and he was two, and I had ridden him ever since. Too tall and with too much Roman nose to be pretty, the gray had three qualities that made him the best horse I ever owned—endurance, sure-footedness, and good sense beyond that of most men. I can't count the times he had saved me grief, and probably saved my life, in the five years we had been together working cattle and covering vast distances on the open prairie. The only other horse I knew that would have a chance in the midst of this blind, pounding avalanche of hides and horns was Clark's quick little catfooted mare, Maude. Both animals seemed to know they wouldn't get a second chance; the first mistake would kill both horse and rider.

Within the first hundred yards I found the stirrups and had my balance. I didn't even try to rein the gray, but gave him slack, letting him run on his own instincts. I felt him working to his left, trying to get clear of the main body of the herd that had swamped us. I could feel the hurtling cattle bumping and banging into us. Time and again he broke the rhythm of his stride to catch his balance and keep running. Even in my panic I felt a surge of gratitude a dozen times at how sure he was on his feet.

I shot a glance behind me to my right, looking for Clark. I couldn't see him, and my heart sank.

After the first two minutes of the stampede my head started to work again. I had to try to get clear of the herd so I could get ahead to turn it. The only way to keep a stampede from scattering cattle all over the country is to get to the leaders and turn them in a circle so they run back to where they started. The gray was working his way out in the clear by his own instinct, but until he broke free, we could only run with them and try to stay alive. Locked in among them it was useless even to *think* of trying to control them.

Some of the cattle stumbled in badger holes, prairie dog holes, on brush and rocks, and some were going down. The ones that did had no chance. Those behind them could neither turn nor stop, and the hundreds of frantic, pounding hooves trampled them into oblivion. I couldn't see the ground and had no idea how the gray knew where to put his feet. But although some of the cattle right around us were going down, the gray was not.

I was suddenly aware there weren't ten cattle between me and the outer edge of the herd. Then five, then two, and then we were running free. I leaned forward, taking the slack out of the reins as I took control of the gray. I touched spur to his flanks, trying to reach the leaders. With his neck out in a straight line and his ears flattened, for more than half a minute he ran harder than he had ever run. I hated to ask him to do it, but we had no choice. We were closing on the leaders fast when suddenly, as if by a signal only they understood, the cattle began to slow. Then they were trotting, and then they stopped—all in a matter of less than a minute. Why they stopped was as much a mystery as why they had started.

I spun the gray to my right to look back. It was light enough now to see the far side of the herd, but I couldn't see Clark. It seemed like my heart stopped. He *couldn't* be down. Not Clark. The gray was blowing hard, trying to catch his wind. I knew he desperately needed time, but again I set both spurs into his flanks, and we went straight back into the herd. With the endurance that made him special he responded. I felt him pushing cattle left and right while my eyes probed for Clark. Suddenly there he was, just coming over a rise, face still white, unable to believe he had somehow survived the stampede.

We shouted and waved. While he was still fifty yards away I yelled, "Have you seen Fritz?" He shook his head no. "Where was he when they started to run?"

Clark was getting close enough for me to see the expression of fear on his face. "I don't know. I hope to God he was on the west side of the herd. If he was on the south end . . ." He didn't finish the sentence.

I spun the gray and we jammed our way back out of the herd. When we were clear I socked the spurs into his flanks one more time, and one more time he hit his running stride in two jumps. We reached the rear of the main part of the herd in less than a minute. The cattle were standing exhausted, not moving, no longer a threat.

I reined in to a trot and worked in to the center of the path of the stampede. I had to take an iron grip on my stomach. It seemed like half the herd was back there dead. Carcasses were strewn over the ground helter skelter, some recognizable, some not. I saw Clark off to my right and behind me, catching up. Half a mile ahead I saw the rest of the crew coming at a lope. Sweet had the Winchester, Lew the double-barreled shotgun. They were all fanned out, coming to see if we were all right. Fritz Hoffman wasn't among them.

Standing in the stirrups and scanning, searching, my eye caught something to my left in a shallow draw in the prairie. I jerked the reins too hard and the gray stopped, his hindquarters skidding just a little.

The buckskin mare Fritz had been riding was standing there, her head down, not moving. I tapped spur, loped the gray over, and pulled to a stop thirty feet away. I sat and stared in disbelief. The saddlehorn was broken and dangling off to one side. The saddle had slipped back maybe eight inches too far behind the withers, hanging at a crazy angle over the ribs. The reins were broken at uneven lengths. She was standing with most of her weight on her hindquarters, just her left front leg touching the ground, the right one held up. It had been broken between the knee and the ankle, and the bone was sticking out through the hide. She had dirt and weeds and hoof marks all over her. Her neck was down, her head nearly touching the ground. She had gone down and been rolled over and over as countless hooves trampled her. How she ever got her feet back under her I'll never know. Even at thirty feet I could see that her eyes were glazed with pain. It was certain she had broken ribs and that some of her inside organs had been punctured. She didn't even know I was there. I stepped off the gray and

walked rapidly to her side. I loosened the cinch, stripped the saddle, blanket, and bridle from her, and dropped them on the ground.

I remounted and was just starting over the north rise of the
little draw to get Sweet's rifle when he appeared, the Winchester
in his hand. He saw what I had done and understood. He went
straight to the mare. With my back turned I heard the cracking
bang of the Winchester. I moved the gray over the rise, backtrack-
ing up the path of the stampede, horrified at what I was going to
find in my search for Fritz. The rest of the crew saw me, and those
nearest turned to follow.

About eighty yards back I found him. He was face down, arms
and legs sprawled out, his right arm at an unnatural angle, badly
broken just below the shoulder. His hat was twenty-five feet
away, dirty and torn. His coat was covered with manure and dirt
and grass and brush, ground in, and it was torn where churning
hooves had kicked and rolled him.

I was aware that others from the crew were coming in, stopping, dismounting, walking toward me. I paid them no heed.
Slowly I walked up to Fritz and knelt down on both knees by his
head. I smoothed back the torn and dirty hair from his face, and
knew he was dead. I stood up and looked down at him, not knowing what to do.

I felt Charlie's hand on my shoulder and I turned toward him.
The crew was all there except for Cookie. I turned back to Fritz
and just looked at him.

None of us professed to be religious, and no one said a word.
One by one we removed our hats and stood there silently, heads
bowed. Twenty minutes ago he had been working with us. But for
the luck of the draw on night duty, that could be any one of us
there on the ground, broken and dead.

We weren't Scots, or Englishmen, or Canadians, looking at a
dead German. We were just men, stripped of all pretenses, looking
at the one certain thing life brings. We had all seen death before,
but out on this lonely, wind-swept prairie, we realized as never
before that when this great leveler of all mankind comes calling,
there is no such thing as nation or race. We are all just men, bound
together by strengths and faults, joy and pain, successes and fail-
ures, and love and dreams. For just a moment, we realized how

much of our lives we spend on things that really don't matter. Looking down at Fritz, torn and dirty and dead, we realized.

Charlie gave us a minute or two with our silent thoughts before he pulled his hat back onto his head. We each put the moment away in a special place in our hearts and minds, to be brought out and examined later. Then we put our hats back on and turned to Charlie for orders.

"We can be thankful they ran south. If they'd come north, they'd have been over the top of us before we got out of our blankets. Sweet and Lew, move out among the cattle that are down and don't let any of them suffer if ye find them alive. Take a count of the carcasses. Henry, ride back to the chuckwagon and bring back a tarp to help me with Fritz. The rest of ye go back to be sure the herd doesn't move. I calculate they ran just under two miles. Anyone disagree?"

We all thought that was about right.

"Anyone know what started 'em?"

No one knew.

"Henry and Clark, where were you when it started, and where did it start?"

I answered first. "We were on the east side at about the middle. I think it started on the north end, over toward the west corner. I got no idea what started 'em." Finished, I looked at Clark.

"I think he's right, Mr. MacDonald. From the time we heard the first sounds until we were in a full flat-out run wasn't more than about two or three seconds. I ain't got no idea what started 'em. I hadn't seen sign of a wolf, but who knows?"

"All right. Let's move out." Charlie started toward his horse. I walked to the gray and patted him on the neck. He had caught his wind and was standing calm, looking at the dead cattle. I lifted his feet one at a time to check the hooves and feel the ankles for any swelling. He seemed to be sound. I pulled his head to me, rubbing his ears and jaws for a minute. I told him out loud he had saved my life and I was grateful. I swear he understood. The men near enough to hear me understood too.

Stepping on, I loped back to the chuckwagon. Cookie gave me some tarp and about thirty feet of soft cotton rope. I stopped at the horse herd to drop my loop on the sorrel and returned to Charlie, leading the sorrel, the tarp under my arm.

We carefully wrapped the body in the tarp, tied it onto the sorrel, and took it back to the chuckwagon. After we unwrapped it I helped Charlie remove the torn, dirty outer coat and the chaps and boots. Using a pan of warm water and soap, the old Scot tenderly washed the bruised, broken face and neck and hands while I dried them with a towel. Then Charlie combed the hair. We laid Fritz back on the tarp and closed and tied it. Cookie rearranged the sacks of flour, potatoes, beans, and sugar in the chuckwagon so we could lay the body just behind the seat.

The weather was cold enough to hold his remains until we could get Fritz back to Raymond. It was only right that his wife and two children should bury him.

While Charlie and I were working on Fritz, I counted sixteen separate booms from the Winchester and the shotgun. Sweet and Lew were finishing their job. As Charlie and I walked to our horses, they came loping in with their report.

"I counted fifty-seven carcasses." Lew looked at Sweet for his count.

"I made it out at fifty-seven too."

I couldn't believe it. I would have sworn there had to be five hundred dead ones. It took me a little time to realize how badly your mind and impressions can trick you when you are under desperate, deadly pressure.

Charlie got out his log and began to write. I had a sense of sympathy for Charlie, knowing the pain he would feel when he sent the report to Fritz' widow and family.

I know he entered the dollar losses right along with the fifty-seven head of cattle. At fifteen dollars a head, that would be another $855 we couldn't bring back to our people. Suddenly I hated thinking of fifty-seven dead cows, one dead buckskin mare, and one dead trail drover as $855 lost. Just for a second I saw my father, furious and preaching to me about six dollars for silver-plated spurs. I had to shake it out of my mind.

Together we rode back to the herd. We were in full daylight now, and we could see the cattle standing, heads down, so tired they weren't moving. Charlie's practical, hard-headed side showed when he spoke to us.

"At least by runnin' south they got us off to a good start for the day. We've already made two miles. We'll need to go back and take the hides from the ones that aren't destroyed too badly. Lew, leave about three men to hold the herd. The rest of ye go and skin out all the hides still worth takin'. Cookie'll be along soon and we'll load the hides on the wagon. We can still make three or four miles this afternoon before dark."

Hides would hold in this weather, and at five dollars each we might get enough to make up for three or four cattle. In my mind flashed the thought, "Six dollars for silver-plated spurs." It wouldn't let go of me.

I was assigned to help hold the herd. I turned the gray south, and as I crested the first rise in the prairie I looked back. I had lived through it, but my mind was still struggling to accept it. From a distance the path of the stampede was all the clearer. On it, scattered at random, were the carcasses, the skinners moving among them looking for hides that could be salvaged. The frozen ground was ripped and pounded so badly it looked like it had been plowed. Every blade of grass, every branch of brush that had been under the pounding hooves was churned into pulp. A feeling rose in me of fear and awe for the terrible, destructive power of the stampede.

About noon the skinners, with the chuckwagon and Cookie, showed up a quarter mile north of the herd. Cookie set about starting the noon meal. The skinners heated some water and peeled off their coats to wash the stench and the blood from their hands. They had taken twenty-one hides; the rest were too damaged to be of any value. At five dollars each it would come to $105. Always, it always had to be translated into dollars. The vision of silver-plated spurs danced through my mind. I had squandered six dollars on silver-plated spurs, while a lot of folks at home were counting pennies. I hated the thought.

It was a pretty quiet meal. Our minds were still struggling with the suddenness and the brutality of the stampede. I know every man there was silently suffering with the question of what would become of Fritz' widow and the newborn son who would never know his daddy.

We took our orders from Charlie in silence. Thirty minutes after we cleaned our plates, we had the cattle up and moving southeast. That afternoon they moved slowly but steadily, and so did we. There was little talk. Our thoughts were back in the predawn darkness, reliving the seven or eight minutes that had turned our world upside down and killed one of us. At dusk we stopped. We hadn't reached the hay drop, but we had found a little pocket of grass. The cattle didn't move ten feet from where they were standing when we turned our horses and quit. Cookie got the cookfire going, and soon the clanging of the triangle called us to our rotation for supper.

While we were eating, Charlie gave us his thoughts. "I don't know if it was wolves started the stampede or not. If it was, it's a good bet they'll stay with the fresh meat we left behind until this drive is over. But, if it was wolves that have learned to love killin' just for the sake of killin', they'll follow. So I'm askin' ye to keep a sharp eye fer the next day or two. We have three, maybe into the fourth day yet to Sweetgrass, and we can't stand another run." We all understood. Charlie knew he didn't have to ask us twice. We didn't want to even think about another stampede.

I was assigned the four-o'clock night duty. I went to my blankets not long after supper, but it was late into the frosty night before my eyes closed. Somehow I started to feel that if I hadn't dozed in the saddle two days before I might have seen the wolf. If I had seen it maybe we'd have done something about it right then. Maybe Fritz would still be alive. I couldn't help it when my thoughts went back to father. Fool's Hill. The king of Fool's Hill. I didn't even know what Fool's Hill was, but if ever anyone felt like the king of Fool's Hill, it was me that night. I drifted into a troubled sleep with a rising feeling of guilt and shame.

Chapter Eight

Just before four in the morning, in cold that made the frost on the ground crackle at every step, I mounted the sorrel and turned her head toward the herd. Today we would cross the Milk River Ridge and continue past the dry bed of the Milk River to the bedground just beyond. By dark we should be just two days from Sweetgrass. We were all daring to feel a little stronger about getting these cattle through to the railroad as we drew closer to the finish. We had survived a blizzard and a stampede, and short of a chinook, which could turn the prairie into a sea of mud, it didn't seem now like much could beat us. Nobody said it, because somehow saying it out loud seemed like an invitation to another disaster. But it was in all our minds.

I felt troubled, unable to clear my mind. I had to concentrate to keep my thoughts on my assignment. I was struggling with the notion that Fritz being dead was connected with me not seeing the wolf, and I couldn't shake loose from it.

I nodded to Joe Swenson coming in and rode to take his place at the edge of the herd. For two hours I rode my position in the dark, watching, listening, talking low to the cattle. My mind wouldn't quit working on the feeling that was growing in my heart that I had broken the rules and Fritz had paid for it.

The predawn streaks of gray came in the east. I was still making my round, watching for anything that moved, feeling the mood of the cattle, talking to them. Suddenly a flicker of movement in the brush to my left brought my head around. The sorrel's head turned too, ears pointing. Her walk stayed steady, but she was looking as hard as I was to see what had moved.

I caught the gray flash again more than 150 yards out, amidst patchy brush. I stopped the sorrel and stood tall in the stirrups, straining. There it was again. This time there was no mistake. I had just seen the head and shoulders of a great gray wolf looking straight at me from between two clumps of brush. The head dropped out of sight just after I stopped to stare back at him.

Something inside me snapped. I was through playing games. Setting my spurs into the sorrel's flanks, I let out a yell that would have scared Geronimo and charged headlong at the brush where I had last seen the wolf. I meant to flush him enough to be sure before going to go tell Charlie. I covered about forty yards at a high run and saw his hindquarters moving away from me over a rise. He stopped long enough to look back at me, puzzled at the sight of a horse and rider coming straight at him at a dead run. Then he was out of sight.

I pulled back on the reins hard enough to set the sorrel on her haunches skidding, then turned her while she was still moving, heading back to the breakfast fire at a run. The men still at the campfire were all on their feet, plates in their hands, faces puzzled at the Indian yell and the sight of me coming in so hard. I reined in and dismounted running while she was still sliding to a stop.

"Mr. MacDonald, I just saw a big gray wolf, tall in the shoulders, probably pretty old. About 150 yards east of the herd, in the brush. Just sittin' there watchin' us. I yelled and charged straight at him to flush him just to be sure, and there ain't no question. He trotted out of sight over a rise but he stopped long enough to look at me. It might be the one you saw."

I was talking faster than usual, still breathing heavy from the run. Charlie's eyes were thoughtful as his mind absorbed the news. A few seconds dragged by. The men were silent, waiting.

"Might be the same one, might not." Charlie's eyes dropped to his plate. I thought he meant to just let it go. I could see the disappointment in the faces of the other men. I couldn't just pass it off, so I moved toward him and spoke.

"Mr. MacDonald, it seems like it might be proper to . . . "

He looked up at me and I stopped, realizing he had meant to continue. "But I think it would be poor judgment to take a chance. If it is the same one, he's here for just one reason." Again he paused. We waited in the silence. "Tommy, ye and Doug get the rifles, and see if ye can find him."

No way was I going to be left out. I had a little something personal to settle with that old gray outlaw. "Mr. MacDonald, I know where he was and which direction he took. I can handle the Springfield good."

I think Charlie realized from the earnest expression on my face how hard I had taken it when he found me dozing in the saddle, and that I somehow felt responsible for losing Fritz. I couldn't leave it to chance. I had to go after the wolf. Throwing all caution and good sense to the wind, I turned to the crew. "There's somethin' else that I got to say."

Every eye in the crew swung to me.

"Three days ago, the afternoon after the blizzard, I was ridin' my position and I fell asleep in the saddle. I don't know how long. Mr. MacDonald found me and woke me up. He'd seen the wolf out not far from me, but because I was asleep, I didn't. Maybe if I'd seen him earlier we would have got him right then. If we had, maybe Fritz would be alive. I ain't goin' to fall asleep any more, but I think you all got a right to know it happened once, and maybe Fritz is dead because of it. I would look mighty kindly on catchin' up with that wolf myself. I don't know what else to say. God knows I'm sorry."

I stopped because there was nothing else to say. I waited with a sense of shame and relief.

"Lad, ye take too much on yerself. Remember. I *did* see the wolf that day, and I judged it didn't merit runnin' him to ground. If there was an error in judgment, it was mine, lad. Life will heap enough of yer own true burdens on ye without takin' on those that belong to someone else."

Charlie wrinkled his forehead and moved his feet a little. "Tommy, take the Winchester. Henry, take the Springfield and start now. Stay within shoutin' distance of each other. If ye haven't finished him by sundown, come back. Do ye understand?"

We understood the assignment. No one will ever know the

weight that lifted from my heart as I turned to take the sorrel back to the horse herd in exchange for the gray.

I heard some of the crew talking as I saddled. It was clear they felt a sense of excitement at the prospect of being rid of the gray ghost that had dogged us for three days, perhaps causing the stampede that killed Fritz.

The old Springfield was so long you couldn't put it in a saddle scabbard. I would have to balance it across my legs behind the saddle bows and hold it with one hand. As I started to mount, Doug approached me.

"Henry, about fallin' to sleep, fergit it. Ain't none of us haven't done that, but most of us never found need to confess. Shoot, I know two, three trailhands that can keep their horse movin' and sing lullabies, all while they're sound asleep. A couple of them can even carry on a good conversation, plumb snorin'. Maybe better than when they're awake. And there ain't no way of knowin' what made the herd stampede. Could have been a nighthawk sneezin' or just anything. We'll never know. Nobody here faults you. Fergit it."

I looked at him and nodded my thanks. It helped me to stop worrying about how the men felt about me, to stop feeling so responsible for Fritz' death.

I swung up on the gray. Tommy stepped onto his bay and we were gone, me leading the way to where the wolf had disappeared less than twenty-five minutes earlier.

We paused on the rise where I had last seen him and leaned over to examine the ground. Our only hope of finding tracks was that he might have stepped in the heavy frost that still held under the grass and brush where the sun hadn't reached.

We found a couple of tracks heading north, angling toward the back of the herd. With hand gestures Tommy indicated he would swing out about a hundred yards. We would walk in the direction the tracks had gone, keeping an eye on the ground, watching for anything moving in the brush ahead of us.

It didn't take us long to find out the old wolf was playing with us. We hadn't gone half a mile, picking up a track in the frost every once in a while, always heading due north, when by pure chance I caught a movement way out to my left. There was old

Lobo, sneaking due south in the brush. I could almost hear him laughing at us.

I waved to catch Tommy's attention and then started to my left, moving the gray to a lope. When we got to where I had last seen him we kept our interval and moved south, again watching, listening. And so it went. Cat and mouse, deep into the afternoon. We were scarcely aware when we climbed the Milk River Ridge, moving down the southeast slope across the dry wash that was the bed of the Milk River.

This old boy had survived by his wits so long that he was smarter than both of us put together when it came to the game of hide and seek. When we moved faster, so did he. When we slowed, looking for tracks or sign, so did he. He didn't move in a straight line for more than fifteen minutes. His changes of direction were sometimes slight, sometimes completely reversed. We knew he was out there, relaxed, using up our horses and time, waiting for us to get tired or disgusted and go back to the herd.

But if we did, it was clear that he would take up his position again, floating at the edge of the herd like a ghost, waiting for a stray or cripple or ready to start another stampede. We were surprised that we didn't see other wolves. It was certain they were out there somewhere—maybe back at the place of the stampede, gorging on the fresh-killed beef. If this old Lobo wanted them, he could cover that distance and have them back here in two hours.

Wouldn't he ever make a mistake? Didn't he ever get overconfident?

I had just turned the gray south again, Tommy swinging around to go with me, when I caught a movement ahead. There he was, on a ridge about four hundred yards out, head down, shoulders high. Then, moving with the smoothness of a shadow as I gazed after him, he turned and disappeared again.

I waved at Tommy as I raised the gray to a lope toward the ridge. There we found some marks on the hard ground that could have been his tracks, but we could only guess which way he went. The sun was getting low. We both knew we were going to have to win this game within half an hour or give up.

We were about two miles east of the herd when Tommy said, "I reckon we better be gettin' back. We'll make the herd just about sundown if we start now. That old boy isn't goin' to be caught by two mounted riders with rifles. It's a sure thing he's out there now watchin' us, just out of gun range. We better turn back."

As he spoke we both sensed a movement to the east. There on a ridge, outlined against the sky, stood the wolf. He was so far away we could barely make it out to be him. His right side was toward us, his head turned our way. He was sure he was out of rifle range. With dark coming on, it seemed like he was saying thanks for the day of fun. He was secure in the notion that we couldn't hurt him over that long distance.

Holding my breath, hoping he wouldn't move, I slowly dismounted and stepped to a little outcropping of rock. With cold fingers I flipped open the rifle breech and dropped one of those great big shells into place. Closing the breech, I snapped the lock and hauled back that monstrous hammer to full cock. In the quiet I thought the two hammer clicks were so loud they would spook him.

Tommy spoke very softly. "I think you got about five seconds, tops, Henry."

"Six hundred?"

"About. At least a long five-fifty."

I snapped the elevator up on the rear sight, moving the slide to the six-hundred-yard mark. I went to one knee, resting the barrel over the rocks as I lined up the shallow notch on the rear sight with the needle-sharp blade of the front sight. I didn't wait. The instant the sights settled on the wolf, I held just a mite high— allowing for the sun behind me shining off the backside of the sights, making them look bigger than they were—and pulled the trigger.

The thundering boom of that old rifle rolled out over the prairie, making our horses flinch and move. I took the shock of the recoil and then jerked my head to look around the cloud of white smoke hanging off the end of the barrel. The bullet would get to the wolf before the sound did, so there would be no boom to warn him.

Tommy was holding his breath, hardly daring to believe a shot from that range could hit what it was aimed at. I know it was only about one full second, but to me it seemed like twenty minutes before things happened. All of a sudden that little speck of a wolf raised up about a foot like he'd been hit with a big fist and tipped over sideways, away from us.

I looked at Tommy, incredulous. "Did it hit him?"

"*Huuuuueeeeee!*" He let out his pent-up breath with a yell. "I think it knocked him rollin'. I don't believe it!"

In the fading light I had to find out if the wolf was down or not. If he was only wounded, we had to find him before dark.

I was back on the gray and turning when Tommy called to me, "You go on. I got somethin' I have to do." I didn't have any idea what he meant.

In my mind I marked the place the wolf had been and rode alone straight to it. He was there, lying on his left side. The big slug had hit him high on the right shoulder. At that range the bullet must have been wobbling, maybe tumbling. It had gone almost all the way through, breaking both shoulders and his spine. He hadn't moved a foot from where he hit the ground.

For a moment I just stood there, trying to tell myself the bullet had hit him. I couldn't repeat that shot in a hundred tries. Then, looking back to signal to Tommy, I blinked in puzzlement.

There he was, leading his bay, taking measured strides, concentrating on the ground. He was walking as straight a line as he could toward me. Why wasn't he mounted?

As he got closer I shouted, "He's here! What do you think you're doing?" There was no answer. He didn't break his concentration but continued staring at the ground and taking measured strides. All I heard, faintly, was "five fifty-*six,* five fifty-*seven,* five fifty-*eight* . . . " He walked past me, counting, and stopped at the wolf. "Five hundred eighty-two yards. With the sunset at your back. Do you think anyone is going to believe that?"

"I don't believe it myself. If it weren't for that hole in him, I'd say he died of a heart attack."

Tommy looked down at the carcass, then back at me. "Your secret is safe with me, Henry. That's exactly what I'll tell 'em. He died of a heart attack and you shot him afterwards to claim the glory."

I grinned, then he grinned, and we both laughed.

I led the gray over so he could see the wolf was dead and wouldn't get jumpy. Then Tommy and I lifted the carcass onto the bedroll behind my saddle, damaged side up, and tied it.

When we rode into camp twenty minutes later, the men who were gathered for supper were waiting for us. They had heard the single blast from the distant rifle and were anxious to hear what had happened. I untied the wolf a little ways away from the horses, letting it drop to the ground.

Charlie was the first one over. "It got so late I thought ye weren't going to get a chance at him. It sounded like the .45-70. Who got him?"

Tommy spoke up. "Henry did. At 582 yards, with the sunset at his back." I looked at Tommy like I had been betrayed, but I couldn't hold back a tight little smile. I basked in the glow of the compliments and wisecracks the guys started to heap on me.

"Henry, just before you got back here, I seen a second wolf off over south of us about four and a half miles. Would you take the Springfield and just step over to that little rise right there and dust him off before it gets too dark?"

"Henry, don't waste no more bullets. Stand up tomorrow mornin' and wave that old Springfield so's the wolves see who it is. They'll just come right on into camp and surrender."

We were all feeling better about things. We had begun to accept the terror of the stampede and the shock of Fritz being dead. The wolf that might have caused it lay dead at our feet. With the Milk River Ridge behind us, the rest of the drive was going to be slightly downhill. The worst of it was behind us, and Sweetgrass was just two or three days ahead. We could all feel our spirits lifting.

I went to my saddlebags and got my big clasp knife to skin the wolf. The hide would bring five dollars when we got back to Raymond. Another five dollars to help just a little to offset the losses we'd had. And this time I had a real glory story to tell father. He'd *have* to be impressed with this one.

It was Cookie who added the final touch. He made a deep-dish apple pie from dried apple slices in the biggest frying pan he had. It had cinnamon and sugar sprinkled over the crust, and none of us could remember a pie to equal it. He set it on the tailgate of the chuckwagon with one of his big spoons stuck in it, intending for us to help ourselves. And we did.

I slept that night with dreams that no longer included a gray wolf that came and went like a ghost. Instead I saw visions of a great, sweet apple pie.

Chapter Nine

Dawn found us talking the cattle off the bedground, crowding them southeast. The routine was familiar by now. They fell into their own natural marching order, the leaders following Lew at point, the others taking a position behind them. They quickly settled into their traveling pace and, strung out, they looked for all the world like a flowing river. For the rest of the day all we had to do was keep crowding them a little.

The weather held sunny but well below freezing. We felt a growing sense of excitement knowing we would probably be in Sweetgrass in two days. Thinking about seeing a new town with new people and being inside of buildings made the hours easier. There was a little extra spring in our step, a little more nonsense and horseplay between us. Our lift in spirits showed, even in the horses. We had passed the last hay drop, but to our surprise there were enough pockets and patches of grass left to keep something in the bellies of the cattle.

Only one thing concerned us. Since we had left the snow, there had hardly been any moisture for the cattle. We had traveled almost two days without enough water. They were showing signs of real thirst, starting to complain with a constant bawling and restlessness. By late afternoon we knew we had to get them to water as fast as we could.

The map showed a natural tank up ahead, a pond big enough to give them all the water they needed. We knew Charlie would get us there in time. After we bedded the cattle for the night, we gathered at supper to listen to him talk about it.

"Lew, about four, five miles up ahead is the tank. I figure it's probably froze over pretty good. It's shallow, only about a foot and a half deep on the average, but big enough to give them all a good watering if we can get it opened up for them. In the mornin' after we get 'em up and movin', let Lee take the point. Ye and Henry go on to the tank ahead of the herd and get the ice broke up at the edges as much as ye can. Take the axe." It was a pretty routine assignment, one that we didn't give much thought to.

The following morning with the cattle up and moving and Lee on point, Lew and I moved out ahead of the herd and angled southeast to the tank. I glanced back for a moment at the sight of the men and the cattle and the vast prairie, the chuckwagon small in the distance. I felt a deep pride and then a stab of sadness, knowing I was looking at a sight that few men would ever see again.

We loped our horses for a couple of minutes, then pulled them down to a walk. We were watching the skyline for the rise in the prairie that we called "the hill." Actually it was little more than a roll that was slightly higher than the others. It was closer than we thought. Within forty minutes we were closing the last quarter mile to the near edge of the tank. As we rode up, our first impression was that we could cut or break the ice along the edges for quite a ways. The cattle would probably break it a little farther back when they began to crowd in.

We dismounted and tested the edges of the ice with our boots. Soon we were several feet out without a sign that the ice would give. Lew walked back to get the axe. We opened a hole in the ice about a foot deep, five feet from shore, but no water.

"Must have been colder here than we figured." Lew looked concerned. "This pond is only about two feet deep, average, and I'm startin' to believe it's froze to the bottom."

He remounted and carefully rode out about three or four feet, ready to turn and get off quick if he heard a crack. There was no sound. He rode a little farther out, but still nothing happened. I could understand the rising concern. If we didn't get through the ice pretty soon we were going to have cattle all over this pond bawling for water, getting hard to handle.

"Henry, ride out here and see if both of us can get a crack in this ice. It looks like this thing is completely frozen."

The two of us, with our rigs and horses, weighed well over a ton. I moved the gray out onto the ice. With his usual good sense he was moving cautiously. Lew was about fifteen feet out. I got within about five feet of him before the world started breaking up.

All around us for thirty or forty feet the ice started to crack with great popping sounds. The horses started to turn even before we pulled rein on them. The gray turned slow enough to keep his feet under him and started walking gingerly back, not trying to run. Lew's brown gelding was terrorized, out of control. He spun too quick and his hooves wouldn't hold on the ice. His hind feet slipped and he came down heavy on his hindquarters, his legs sprawling, scrambling for control. The sudden impact of fourteen hundred pounds of horse and rider hitting the ice finished the cracking we had started. His hindquarters went through the ice amidst a shower of ice shards and water. My back was to Lew when it happened but I heard it, both the cracking and the sudden eruption of ice and water when the horse went through. I turned the gray as his front feet came onto frozen prairie, expecting to see Lew sitting on his horse up to its knees in water in the shallow pond.

I wasn't prepared for the near panic that surged through me. We must have ridden out over a deep hole in an otherwise shallow pond. The horse's hindquarters were clear out of sight. All I could see back of his neck was the horn of the saddle. With his front feet still on the ice, the brown had almost reared over backward, and Lew had partially thrown himself to his left to keep from being pinned under in the water in case the horse came clear on over. He didn't quite tip over, but in the desperate scramble Lew had been thrown into the water clear to his chin. The horse went crazy with fear. His back legs couldn't touch bottom, leaving him scrambling to pull himself up onto the ice with his front legs. Lew, realizing the hopelessness of getting control of the horse, kicked his left foot out of the stirrup so he could get disengaged. In the struggle his head went clear under.

Quickly I shook a loop out in my lariat. As Lew came back to the surface, my lariat dropped over his head and shoulders. He grabbed the rawhide and I took two quick dallies around the saddlehorn, turned the gray, and started slowly away from the pond. I didn't want to jerk Lew against jagged ice that could cut him or break bones. He didn't try to get his feet under him until I had him on the ground. Then he got one knee under him as I dismounted and started for him to help take the lariat off.

The temperature was about an even zero in frigid sunlight. Already ice had begun to set up in Lew's week-old beard. His matted hair and clothes began to stiffen. His hat was still in the water. He started back, intent on doing something to get the horse out before it froze to death or hurt or killed itself fighting the great floating sheets of broken ice.

But I knew we would never get the horse out before Lew froze to death. I vaulted back onto the gray, holding my left leg well ahead of the stirrup, offering it to Lew. "Lew. Get up here. We got about ten minutes before you freeze to death. Move!"

Lew couldn't stand to leave the horse there. I hated it too, but there wasn't a thing we could do about it. I *had* to get Lew up on the gray.

"Lew, get up here. *Now!*" I reined the gray up so the side with the exposed left stirrup was jammed right into Lew's chest. I reached down and grabbed the back of his greatcoat collar, stiff with ice, and jerked as hard as I could. He had little choice. He could barely raise his left foot to the stirrup but with me pulling and him giving what little strength he had left, we managed to get him up behind me. I reached around and grabbed his right arm with mine so he was partly holding onto me. When I felt his left hand come up under my other arm, I knew he had a full hold on me.

I turned the gray north and set the spurs. Carrying double, the horse settled into a run. I held him back enough so he could hold the pace for the full distance back to the herd. The gray was paying the price to get Lew back to help before he got frostbitten or died. His steadily drumming feet ate up the distance. I calculate we ran more than two miles. I didn't come in shouting because I didn't want to stop the cattle or scare the trailhands. When they saw me coming in riding double, they watched me all the way to the chuckwagon.

Charlie rode to meet me at a run. I waved to him, holding my pace until I got to the chuckwagon. Cookie stopped the chuckwagon just as Charlie got there. I let go of Lew's arm so Charlie could help him down onto his feet.

I spoke first, still mounted. "Lew went through the ice on that shallow pond that ain't shallow, clear out of sight. About fifteen feet from shore. I pulled him out. There wasn't anything there to build a fire with in a hurry, so I brought him back. If you and Cookie can get his clothes off him and get some blankets onto him, maybe start a fire and get something hot inside him, I think he'll make it."

I dismounted and grabbed my bedroll from the chuckwagon. "Here's my bedroll and blankets to help wrap him. Cookie, get me the Winchester. If you two can take care of him, I got to go back for the horse. It was still thrashin' around out there amongst big sheets of ice. I hated to leave him, but I had no choice."

Cookie reached for the rifle from beside the chuckwagon seat as I remounted. "Mr. MacDonald, will you be all right here with Lew?" I asked.

Charlie nodded, still working to take off Lew's icy, stiff outer coat. I touched spur and reined the gray toward the front of the chuckwagon, where Cookie handed me the rifle as I passed. I headed back the way I had come, raising the gray to the same steady run that had carried Lew and me from the pond.

I dreaded what I was going to find. As I crested the last rise I set my jaw, expecting to find the horse either dead in the water, or almost dead, still trying to heave himself up onto an ice sheet that wouldn't give him footing. I was sure I would have to shoot him if he was still alive.

My heart came right up into my throat at what I saw. Somehow the horse had fought and struggled and broken his way through the ice to the shore. I don't know if he finally got his hind feet out of the hole onto the bottom of the pond, so he could buck-jump and fight his way out, or if he did it some other way. All I know is that when I crested that last rise four hundred yards from the pond, there he came, trotting due north on his way back to the herd, reins dragging, holding his head to one side so he wouldn't step on them and break them.

He knew I had come to help. He let me ride right up to him. I dismounted for the few seconds it took to rub my hand down his sides. There was a bad cut on his chest where some jagged ice had broken through the hide during his struggle. I ran my hand over each leg to be sure they were all sound. Ice had formed all over him; the saddle was slick with it.

With the brown's reins in my hands, I swung back onto the gray and set off again for the herd, raising both horses to an easy lope. The best chance for the brown was to keep his blood running, to keep him warm. We covered the two miles in good time, holding a gentle lope all the way.

Lew was all bundled up in six or eight blankets on the tailgate of the chuckwagon, holding a cup of steaming coffee. Cookie had built a huge fire and hung the frozen clothes nearby to thaw and dry. I reined up close to the fire and stripped the saddle from the brown. Cookie and I each took an empty burlap potato sack and began to rub him down, getting the ice off, starting to dry him.

Charlie stepped over and took the sack from me. "Tend the gray, lad." I went back to the gray and walked him around for a couple of minutes to let him cool slow. Then I got another sack and gave him a good rubdown, standing near the fire. Cookie made a warm gruel from rolled oats and hot water, then laced it with just a little whisky from the medicine chest. Both horses stuck their noses into it and gratefully ate it all. We rubbed some warm salve into the cut on the brown's chest to help start the healing.

With my first chance to pause, I walked over to Lew. "You all right?"

He grinned, embarrassed. "No, but I will be as soon as my pride heals." He paused for a minute, noisily sipping at the steaming coffee. "I hate to think of what would have happened if we had both gone through that ice." I hadn't even thought about that. As I pondered it, I wondered too.

"Tell the gray horse thanks for me, next chance you get."

"I already did. And the gray said you're right welcome, any time."

Charlie interrupted. "What condition are we in for water at the tank?"

"I think you'll have about eighty or ninety feet of open water on the near side. Big sheets broke off in both directions when the horse went through."

"That ought to be enough," Charlie said. "I better get up with the herd. Ye stay with the wagon, Henry. Catch up as soon as Lew and the brown can travel." He mounted and turned south. We waited a while before bundling Lew into the back of the chuckwagon, his damp clothes inside a tarp beside him. Cookie started rolling south and we caught up with the herd an hour later. The cattle were milling around the water tank at the side where the ice had been broken.

Within a couple of hours they had their fill. We moved them almost two more miles south before dusk set in.

Cookie made an extra-large cookfire that night so we could put the damp clothes back out to dry. At supper the crew gathered around the fire to eat while Lew and I told them the story. After we finished, the guys began to work it over and retell it. They added little embellishments—a word here, a thought there. I knew we had brushed close to death that day, but I had to laugh despite myself. If you looked at the humorous side of it and made just a few alterations, it became the craziest, funniest story of the entire cattle drive.

"Ain't it a marvel what the human brain can dream up to get out of doin' a day's work?"

"Lew, if you'da just said somethin', we woulda let you sit in the chuckwagon wrapped in blankets drinkin' coffee all day without goin' through all the nonsense. Why, we can work out a regular rotation on that, each of us takin' a turn."

"Lew, next time you get the waterin' assignment, get a pencil and paper and we'll draw you a picture on how to go about it."

"You expectin' to draw regular pay fer this or are you buckin' fer a raise?"

"Come spring, a couple of us'll give you some lessons on swimmin', Lew."

As Lew listened to the way the guys were finally telling it, he was chuckling right along with them. I was putting together my own version to tell at home so father and Elmer would know my part in it and be impressed.

The humor continued for a while before it died down. It was Tommy who put it to rest with the final word before we went to our blankets. "Mr. MacDonald, you might want to make a note in your logbook. Next time you send Henry and Lew out to the tank to get water, make sure they got a bar of soap."

Chapter Ten

In the predawn darkness Charlie gave us orders for the day while we ate our breakfast.

"Sweet, I calculate Sweetgrass is about six or seven miles south and east of here. Start now. Find whoever's in charge of the Great Northern Railroad office, and tell him we're coming in this afternoon with about twenty-eight hundred head of range stock, heifers and steers. He should have got a telegram about it a day or two after we left. Find out if the railroad cars are there and when we can load. Take a look at the loading chutes to see how many they got. Find out how many cattle pens they got, and the water and feed arrangements, so we'll know where we can hold the herd until they're all loaded. I expect ye can be back and meet us in about four, five hours."

Sweet nodded as he turned to go. We couldn't miss his grin or the spring in his step. We all felt the anticipation and excitement of reaching Sweetgrass. We knew we would each have a little time in town among new people, seeing new things. But most of all we knew it would mark the successful completion of a daring, desperate gamble that might save all our homes and families.

We moved into the herd a little stronger, a little more eager, getting them up and moving by sunrise. We knew Sweet couldn't get back much before noon, but by ten o'clock we were constantly glancing southeast hoping to see his silhouette on the skyline.

We were standing by the chuckwagon just finishing our noon meal when he came loping in. He dismounted, smiling, and made his report to Charlie.

"We're about three miles out right now, maybe a little over. We got open ground all the way in. They never got the word until yesterday because the blizzard busted down the telegraph lines. They got about twenty cattle cars on the siding now, with forty more comin' in from Havre day after tomorrow. They got pens for about five hundred head, all empty, but with twenty-eight hundred head they recommend we hold 'em all in a natural little pocket about a half mile from town, out in the open. I think they're right. They got about sixty tons of grass hay out there sittin' in three stacks, left over from the heavy shippin' season last fall. They'd be glad to sell it to us for just about nothin'—maybe ninety dollars American for the whole load. I told 'em we'd take it. They also got three big waterin' troughs out there hooked up to wind-mills, and they're thawin' out the tops of the lines right now. Should be runnin' water before we get back. They got three loadin' chutes on the siding, spaced so you can load three cars at a time. They got a yard manager, a big black man named Abra-ham, seems to know what he's doin'. He's waitin' to help us get settled in right now."

"What kind of a reception did ye get?" Charlie's expression didn't change, but he couldn't hide the light that came into his eyes. "Any trouble, any problems with any of the townspeople?"

"No, just the other way around. The Great Northern agent has the post office and the telegraph office right there in his ticket office. Runs all of 'em—it's right by the general store, which is also the hotel and cafe. The whole town knew we were comin' after Baker's telegram got through yesterday. I no sooner finished tellin' him who I was when he asked me if there really were ten men crazy enough to trail drive twenty-eight hundred head of range cattle down across the Milk River badlands in the middle of January. He said it like a compliment. I told him yes and that we were comin' in with the herd. When we got through with our business, he walked with me into the general store next door, and before you knew it everyone in town knew the whole deal. I guess thirty people must've stepped outside to look at me as I passed, just wonderin' what a certified crazy man looks like."

Sweet was grinning, enjoying every minute of it. "It wouldn't surprise me if we met a welcomin' committee comin' out to meet us. I know the word is out to some of the local ranches. Some of the ranch hands will likely show up for a day or two."

"How big is Sweetgrass now?" Charlie asked. "Grown much?"

"I don't know how big it was before. I judge it about like Raymond. A bank and a saloon and the general store. A schoolhouse off to one side and a church. A livery and a blacksmith shed and some houses. All of it needs paintin'. I expect close to two hundred live in town."

Charlie cleaned his plate, ready to move on. Sweet stopped him. "I should also mention the whole town is sufferin' from cabin fever. Our comin' in is providin' the only break from monotony and boredom they've had for two months, barrin' Christmas. I expect we can get volunteers to hold the cattle for nothin', just because they ain't had nothin' to do since the freeze set in. We're goin' to be welcome, Mr. MacDonald."

Charlie knew that in a roundabout way Sweet was asking for a little time off for the men, so we could go into town for a change of scenery and people. He handed his plate to Cookie and then turned back to us. The beginnings of a smile tugged at the corners of his mouth.

"Follow Sweet to the bedground outside of town. I'll make assignments at supper after the cattle are bedded. Tomorrow we'll work things out for holding the cattle until they're loaded. Once they get to the grass hay and the water, I don't imagine they'll need any attention. I think we can find a little free time. Mind your manners; we don't want any trouble."

The men grinned in anticipation. I doubted anyone would get into real trouble, but sometimes their love for fun and action needed a little understanding.

We started the cattle moving. About midafternoon Lew signaled, and we knew he was looking down the slight incline toward Sweetgrass. Soon the flowing carpet of hides and horns was on the incline and moving steadily down. Each of us relished the sight of Sweetgrass; it was just as Sweet had described it. Half a dozen mounted riders came toward us, took off their hats while they spoke to Lew, then turned and loped back to the townspeople, who were standing in three or four groups watching us come in.

Ten men crazy enough to bring twenty-eight hundred cattle through the Milk River badlands in January. That's what the agent had said. We were finishing something that would be talked about for quite a while. We sat a little straighter and reined the horses a little smarter.

Sweet was up with Lew, pointing past the town. Following the direction of his extended arm, we saw the little pocket he had described with the stacked hay and the windmills and watering troughs. Lew corrected his angle, turning the cattle just a little north of town within about a hundred yards of the nearest buildings. We passed close enough to tip our hats to some of the people, who waved back.

Charlie and I were riding drag as usual. When we were maybe two hundred yards past the outskirts of town, the sound of a running horse and a voice behind us brought us both around. One of the townspeople was pretty upset about something as he pulled his horse in beside us. "There's a great big steer in town runnin' up and down the main street, scarin' folks and bustin' things up. You better come get him quick, or someone's goin' to shoot him sure."

We both knew exactly which steer he was talking about. He had given us trouble before.

Charlie yelled to Clark Lund, who was riding flanker to our right. Clark came running when he caught the urgency in Charlie's voice. "Clark, take Henry and go back to town. Move that big spotted steer, the herd-quitter that's been runnin' all over the country since the blizzard, on down to the cattle pens and lock him up."

Clark didn't even slow down. I reined around and fell in beside him, and the man from town followed us back. We didn't know it as we rode in, but what took place the next seven or eight minutes was going to be buzzed about for days and talked about for years to come.

We came in on the east end of the dirt main street. Up at the other end, trotting from side to side, head high and ears pointing, charging around like he was insane, was the big spotted steer. Three or four years ago when he was dragged to the branding fire, they had notched his ear, branded him, castrated him, and then nipped his stubby horns. But they hadn't nipped them quite close enough to get the quick and stop their growth. The blunt-ended horns had grown out again about a foot and a half on each side, and the steer had grown to past eighteen hundred pounds. He was tall in the shoulders, horns about four feet from tip to tip, ready to fight anything that moved.

Everybody up at that end of town had been scared inside the buildings. They watched as the steer busted through the board sidewalk here and there and tipped over a couple of barrels and packing boxes that sat outside.

Loping up the street, we slowed to a walk when we got closer, talking to him quiet, trying to settle him. When he spotted us coming in, his head jerked around. His ears pointed straight at us. He was ready for war. He pointed his nose at Clark and charged straight at him, his hooves tearing up dirt for thirty feet.

Clark reined Maude to his left and the steer missed. As he went past, Clark was shaking out his lariat. He spun Maude; the steer skidded to a stop, spun, and came roaring back, making all the sounds of a freight train. I was shaking my loop out too—but big as he was and hard as he was running, I was also thinking about a way out in case he changed his mind about killing Clark and came after me.

Clark waited until the steer was about thirty-five feet out. Then he tapped his spurs, and in two jumps Maude was at a high run, heading right at the steer. At the last second Clark did some maneuvering the like of which I hadn't seen before and haven't since.

He reined Maude just a mite to the left and the steer missed again. But as he passed, Clark dropped his loop over the horns with as neat a backhand move as I have ever seen. He let go of the coil of the lariat and reined Maude back to her right a little, at the same time taking two dallies around the saddlehorn with his end of the lariat. He pulled Maude to a skidding stop and they both looked over their right shoulders, calculating when the steer would hit the end of the lariat. Clark kept Maude pointed at an angle away from the steer. That way she could take most of the jolt on her right side, back over her hindquarters, which was her best chance to keep her feet. Clark kicked his right foot free of its stirrup, hooked his spur under the skirt of the saddle on the right side, and hung there on Maude's left side, all his weight in the left stirrup. Maude sort of spraddled her hind legs out, getting set.

All that happened in less than two seconds. I wasn't moving; I felt struck dumb by what I was seeing. If it had been up to me to stop the steer at that moment, he'd have killed me and the gray and wrecked the whole town before I could have gotten my mind back into the fight. Watching Clark function was like watching a story in action.

With his size and weight, the steer was used to having his own way with just about anything. This was no exception. He knew what it meant when the lariat dropped over his horns. But running straight away from Clark and Maude, he figured to just lower his head and jerk them both down, then come back to work them over with his feet and horns.

Then he hit the end of the lariat. If I live to be a hundred I'll never forget the few seconds that came next.

Clark timed it perfectly. At the instant the lariat took all the shock, Clark and Maude leaned even farther left. I thought Maude was going to fall over, but she kept her feet. I expected the rawhide lariat to break, but it was singing tight, running in a straight line from the saddlehorn right up the steer's back to his horns. It jerked his head straight back and lifted him straight into the air, his nose rising to about eight or nine feet. As his body passed underneath his head, his nose pointed back up the lariat toward Clark while his tail pointed directly away. His body was parallel to the ground about four feet high, his feet straight up in the air.

For just a moment in time it seemed like he hung there exactly upside down. Then he dropped straight to the ground. When he hit, the earth shook. You could hear his grunt clear up to Canada. He lay there for a second with the wind knocked out of him, not able to figure out how the world and the sky got mixed up. I came back to my senses, loped the gray in, and dropped my loop on his horns before he got up, taking my dallies about fifteen feet from his head. Clark quickly unwrapped his dallies, moved Maude to about fifteen feet on the opposite side, and took new ones. Then we spread out—Clark on one side, me on the other.

We had him.

We gave him just enough slack so he could heave himself to his feet when he finally got the ground and the sky separated to their proper places. His first notion was to charge right back up the street, but we both jerked him back between us. Every time he tried to throw his head, or turn, or start busting up and down the street again, we spread our horses until both ropes were tight. He couldn't get enough leverage to do anything but follow us where we took him.

We walked him down to the cattle pens at the edge of town where Abraham, the yardman left in charge for the winter, was waiting. He opened the gate as we approached to let the steer know we meant to put him inside. The steer set all four feet forward, stiffening his legs to do all he could to keep from being penned. We touched spur to the horses and dragged him the last fifty feet, and his hooves cut little furrows in the frozen ground like it had been plowed. After we got him inside, Abraham walked right up to him and started to work the loops loose.

I was scared of what would happen when the steer was loose. As Abraham dropped the last loop to the ground, he reached out to swat the steer's face with his leather fur-lined cap, the ear flaps and tie string flapping.

The blunted horns didn't bother him at all. "Ah ain't skeered a these critters less'n they got full-growed horns." He turned and walked away from the steer; the animal just looked at him until he walked through the gate and closed it. I couldn't believe my eyes.

"Gennelmen, less'n you prefer it otherwise Ah'll jes hold this animal heah until we loads up day aftuh tomorra. Ah thank you both kindly for your assistance."

Clark and I both mumbled our thanks as we turned to go, nearly speechless at how casual Abraham was with a killer like the big spotted steer. I had seen a couple of black men in my life, but it surprised me to find this one here, with his deep, funny, soft Southern accent, holding cattle in the middle of a Montana winter.

Clark and I rode back to report to Charlie before we returned to our positions with the herd. I knew I had seen the finest bit of roping I would ever see in my life. It was going to make one great story for the supper fire, and an even better one to use on father.

The next day, half the town wanted to see Clark. To hear them tell it, he had saved Sweetgrass. He could do things with a rope and horse that hadn't even been invented yet. I had to agree. It gave me real pleasure to see him, as shy as he was, grinning a red-face grin but enjoying the thought that others recognized his one great talent.

When that trail-weary herd walked up to the hay and water, they thought they had gone to heaven. It did us all a lot of good to watch them getting their fill of decent feed and water for the first time in more than two days.

Charlie left Lew in charge while he rode back to town. He had to talk with the railroad agent about shipping arrangements, and with the store owners to see what damage the steer had done. Half an hour later he returned to give us our orders for the night.

"The townspeople wouldn't take money for the damages the steer did, which was about fifteen dollars. They were too busy talkin' about Clark and Henry ropin' him. Tonight I want to hear what ye did with that rope, Clark. Regardin' the cattle, sometime tomorrow afternoon the forty cars from Havre will get here. We can't load in the dark because we have to take an accurate count, so we'll start loadin' in the mornin' day after tomorrow. I imagine Sweetgrass goes to bed with the sun, with the possible exception of the saloon. So if you'll check with Lew, he has a couple of dollars' advance on yer wages if anyone wants to go in tonight fer a social hour or so. Mind yer manners and no trouble. Be sure yer back here by around ten o'clock."

Joking and joviality ran rampant while the crew finished supper. Each man walked over to Lew for a little pocket money, which he gave them gladly. In groups of two and three they rode into town for an evening of friendly hoorahing. By eleven o'clock they were all back, talking quiet and laughing, enjoying being free of the responsibility for twenty-eight hundred cattle for the first time in two weeks. I didn't have any business in the saloon, so I took first duty night herd. Just after midnight Bill Ackersley came to replace me and I went back to the chuckwagon to get my bedroll.

I rolled into my bedroll for the night knowing that a man never sleeps sounder than when he has just successfully finished a tough, desperate, chancy job.

Chapter Eleven

I was up with the sun. I pulled on my hat and boots, peeled back the blankets, and made up my bedroll. At the chuckwagon I greeted Cookie with a "good mornin'," which he returned with that funny grin of his. As usual he had his breakfast fire going, but this time the great skillet was full of scrambled fresh eggs one of the men had brought from town. Beside it, a griddle was heaped with slowly crisping bacon. The two-gallon coffee pot was boiling, steam rising from the spout straight into the air. There's something special about the smell of bacon and eggs and coffee being cooked out in the open on a still, frosty, clear morning. Cookie was humming a sort of twangy, singsong little melody that sounded like it had a lot of pigtailed Chinese folks in it somewhere. With my plate filled, I stood at the fire eating and joshing with the others, feeling good about being there, enjoying being around Cookie.

I cleaned my utensils and dropped them into the kettle of steaming water to be washed and put back in the box in the chuckwagon. I saddled the sorrel and made a slow circle around the herd. One thing was sure. We wouldn't have to watch the cattle today. With good feed and water and the little pocket that gave them some protection from winds, they weren't going to move.

Charlie and most of the crew were still standing around the fire finishing Cookie's eggs and bacon, talking, swapping big lies

about anything they could think of, making plans for the day.
Charlie raised his eyes to me as I rode up. "Lad, ye didn't take time
in town last night. If ye like, go ahead now. Be back fer the noon
meal. And stay away from strong drink and women. I promised
yer mother I'd be responsible."

He was smiling. He knew the one thing he didn't have to worry
about was me getting mixed up with strong drink and women. I
grinned back at him. "Mr. MacDonald, I think I'm going into town
and drink it dry and chase every woman I can find plumb up to
the international border."

Charlie looked startled for a moment, then broke out laughing.
It was the only time I had ever seen him really laugh. I was
grinning and the crew was laughing with him.

I took a minute to wash my hands and face again and combed
my hair. When I put my hat back on I couldn't see that my efforts
made any difference at all, except I felt I had met all the social
requirements for going into town.

I trotted the sorrel to the west end of the main street, then
pulled her down to a walk. I bid a good morning to a few people
as I rode up the main street. I dismounted in front of the general
store, thinking I'd see if there was something I could buy for the
folks at home.

Inside, a few ladies were talking while they picked out canned
goods and other items. Spices, cabbage, and a barrel of dill pickles,
and smoked hams and bacon hung from hooks toward the back of
the store, all added to the special pungency of the atmosphere. On
shelves along one wall were stacks of new denim jeans, shirts, and
bolts of checkered cloth. In one back corner was a rack of rifles
and shotguns, a few handguns, and a stack of ammunition. By the
cash register a glassed-in case held candies, most of them hard,
all of them wrapped. There were a few sacks of potatoes and
onions standing near the door next to apples in a box. Throughout
the rest of the store were all the other necessaries for living on the
frontier—axe handles and shovels and hoes; boots and spurs; a
saddle and some bridles and saddle blankets; flour and sugar and
lard; all things imaginable. The blend of sights and smells was
rich and fascinating.

On a shelf above the sacked potatoes stood fifty or sixty books
of various sizes and shapes on all kinds of subjects. I couldn't

resist them. One of the bigger ones had a drawing of a great big sailing ship on the cover. Inside were stories of the great explorers who sailed the seas hundreds of years ago. I guess I got lost reading about the faraway places they visited and the strange, fascinating people they met. I don't know how long I stood there before a pleasant lady wearing a large apron asked if she could help me find something.

I went red-faced with embarrassment, knowing I probably shouldn't be standing there reading their books. "Yes, ma'am, er—no, ma'am. I was sort of looking around. I wanted to find something to take back home to my brother and maybe my mother and father. If it's all right with you, I'll just look around for a minute."

She smiled, understanding. "How long do you think you'll all be in town?"

"Maybe 'til tomorrow, ma'am. We'll load the cattle out and then probably be on our way."

"Take your time. If there's anything you want to know about, ask Mr. Bjornson over there."

I noticed for the first time a man who stood by a door marked OFFICE at the back of the store behind the smoked meat. He was well over six feet tall, but it was his weight that startled me. I've been judging the weight of beef all my life, and I'll bet that man weighed 380 pounds on the hoof. He was massive.

I nodded to him and he bobbed his head back at me, his shrewd eyes sizing me up.

I spent a little more time in the store, wandering past everything and smelling all the pleasant smells, getting the feel of this new and interesting place. When I finished I said my thanks to the woman and left. I walked a few steps down the board sidewalk, looking at the few people on the street enjoying the clear, windless sky and the warmth of the sunshine in the freezing air. The railroad office was right close by, so I went in. In response to my question the clerk said the railroad cars from Havre would be in late today, maybe tonight. He treated me with respect, knowing I was part of the crew that had brought the cattle in.

I sauntered on down the street, enjoying the quiet of the little town. I walked into the lobby of the hotel and was surprised when some of the people inside greeted me, recognizing me as part of the cattle crew. I returned the greeting and sat down near the big front window to watch the world go by for a while. A couple of the men came over to ask questions about the drive. It seemed a sort of festive spirit was creeping into town. It all had to do with the arrival of the herd, Clark's roping, and the fact that some of our crew had been in town last night laughing with the townspeople and telling stories from the drive.

Finally I walked slowly back to the sorrel. As I left town, three of the crew were coming in. I raised a finger to my hat brim and smiled as I passed. John Sweet grinned that carefree, reckless grin. "Mind the herd, Henry. We'll be back about one o'clock."

I continued back to the windmills and the hay and water and the familiar sounds and smells of cattle. I spent a little time at the chuckwagon watching Cookie get ready for the midday meal. I think he wondered why I was hanging around, but he continued his work, seeming to enjoy having someone there who appreciated what he was doing.

"Cookie, you want to go into town? Let me do some of this stuff for you. You take my horse and go on in. You'll like it. You'll like the general store."

He smiled until his slanted eyes almost closed, shaking his head no. He pieced together a few English words to respond. "Can't not do. Fix glub." "Glub" was the best he could do when he tried to say "grub." He was too shy, too uncomfortable among strangers to go into town, but I could tell it pleasured him to have someone offer, to let him know we appreciated him and thought about him.

Before long he banged on the triangle and the crew started coming in. About one o'clock all of us except the three who were in town had finished the midday feed. Charlie was hunkered down not far from me, cleaning his plate with a piece of sourdough bread when we heard the drumming of a loping horse coming from the direction of town.

We stood and looked. Sweet was coming in at a lope. From the set of his jaw we knew something unusual was happening. Charlie set his plate down as Sweet dismounted.

Sweet gave me a head sign to get on over, pronto. I walked over with a growing feeling that there was trouble.

"What's doin'?" Charlie was clearly puzzled and concerned.

"Mr. MacDonald, we got a situation in town and we got to get right back in to handle it. In the saloon they got a few tables for dominoes and cards and checkers. There's this one jasper thinks he's a champeen checkers player. Ackersley sat down with him, and with table stakes at a dime a game, Ackersley lost twenty cents to him. Ackersley just wanted to play checkers. Winnin' or losin' didn't mean a thing to him, so he just paid off and thanked the guy. We didn't think nothin' more about it."

Sweet stopped to shift his feet and order his thoughts before continuing. "Then this joker gets his jaw loosened up, and we soon learned that if he ain't the world champeen checkers player he's sure the world champeen manure spreader. He comes on like it's too bad the entire Nation of Canada hasn't got nobody that can play checkers in his league, and he'd sure like to have someone come on down that could at least make a game interesting for him before he beat 'em."

It was becoming clear that Sweet's fighting blood was rising. "Now this rolls off me and Ackersley pretty easy, so I signaled to Bill for us to just quietly mosey out of there, which Bill does. On the way out I mentioned to him that we got a man in this crew that can beat him."

Sweet gave us just a second to digest that one. "This gent, his name's Jack, looks at me with that big toothy grin of his and says somethin' like 'Of course you do. Ain't it too bad he just can't take the time to come in here and prove it?' I didn't say nothin' and left with Bill. Bill went on over to the general store to find Doug, and I came here."

Charlie looked at the ground and I stared at Sweet, both of us trying to piece this together and make sense of what Sweet was coming to.

"As I see it, we got sort of a patriotic duty to take Henry back in there and let him whup this guy in a checkers game, Mr. MacDonald."

There it was, simple and clear. Sweet dropped it on me so fast I couldn't catch up with him for a minute or two. *I* was the one supposed to go in there and beat Toothy Jack! Maybe beating J.W. Brewerton back in the Raymond pool hall when I was ten wasn't such a good idea after all. I didn't mind being thought of as the local checkers authority up there, because it didn't amount to much. But being singled out to take on the local hero here was something else again.

By the way Sweet rode and looked coming from town, we all thought something really bad was going on. Now it seemed like this desperate problem boiled down to the nonsense of whether or not we had someone in the crew who could beat the local braggart at checkers. Sweet probably did want to see someone beat this loudmouth. But it seemed he also saw a chance to build a simple game of checkers into something the whole town could get lathered up about, to break the monotony of a long, cold Montana winter. I think if Sweet had an extra day, he would have roped the Governor into this and parlayed it into the International Checkers Championship. It didn't really matter much who won; the whole idea was that the crew and the town were just looking for an excuse to whoop and holler a little and howl at the moon that night. I had to grin at the genius I was seeing in Sweet.

Charlie and the rest of the crew knew about me and checkers, and I could sense their blood rising to the occasion. I tried to read Charlie's face.

"Can ye keep this whole thing under control? I mean, after Henry wins this game will there be any hard feelin's or trouble?"

I looked at Charlie in shock. *After Henry wins this game?* It never seemed to enter Charlie's head that I might lose. It scared me when I realized it.

"Win, lose, or draw, the crew ain't goin' to be nothin' but gennelmen, Mr. MacDonald. This here tournament can go a long way towards improvin' international relationships."

Charlie shook his head, acknowledging his inability to keep up with Sweet's schemes.

"One more thing," Sweet said. "I don't reckon there's much reason the whole crew can't come on down for this, seein' how these cattle are settled in for the next day or two. What do you say, Mr. MacDonald?"

Charlie looked at the herd. It was true; no one was needed here for the next little while.

"Am I considered part of this crew for purposes of viewin' this competition?" Charlie looked serious.

"Chairman and chief bottle washer of the Canadian Delegation, Mr. MacDonald." Sweet looked just as serious as Charlie.

By now everyone was gathered around except Ackersley and Doug, who were still in town. Even Cookie stood quietly to one side, trying to understand. The whole bunch was starting to catch the spirit of this thing, and it was plain they couldn't wait to see if I could win. I was feeling competition rise in my system, too.

Charlie started for his horse. "Then I reckon the Canadian Delegation better make its presence felt, Sweet."

Ten minutes later we were all tying our horses to the hitchrack in front of the saloon. They hadn't asked Cookie to come; they just saddled a horse and put him on and brought him. He didn't resist. He was taking as much pleasure in this as they were. Nor did any of them ask me if I wanted to play checkers. Of *course* I was going to play checkers.

Sweet led the way inside and made introductions. I got a look at Jack and kept an eye on him while we got past the formalities, trying to figure out if he was a thinker or all mouth. I decided he could probably play pretty good checkers but his biggest talent was talking.

We worked out the rules. Everyone was to remain quiet during play. Jack and I were to be seated next to the window. House rules applied to betting; one dime per game per customer. Two out of three games would decide the winner. Standard checkers rules.

We set up the board and began.

There are two general approaches to playing checkers. You can move your men up the middle of the board in a sort of spearhead shape, and pick off the opponent's men on either side of you. Or, you can move your men up both sides, leaving a pocket in the middle, and pick the opponent off from both sides. It all depends on what the opponent does with his first two or three moves. Reading those moves is the key to how you play and whether you win.

I knew when I sat down that Jack was making a bad mistake. He was studying me real close. I was dressed in full gear, including boots and spurs, heavy chaps, an inside coat and the heavy brown wool one, leather gloves, my blue wool scarf, and the big wide-brimmed high-crowned hat with a crease up the front. To him, I looked like sort of a runty little kid trying to play like a man. He looked at my face, smooth cheeked and young, and concluded we were making sport of him, bringing in this kid just to insult him.

The first game was over on the fourteenth move. It lasted less than five minutes. He looked up embarrassed and shocked at getting beat while we set up the men again.

The second game was even shorter, ending on the thirteenth move. I had beaten him twice.

He looked at me in disbelief. I wondered if he was enough of a sport to take a licking from a smart-aleck kid in front of this crowd. He pushed himself back from the table and stuck out his hand to shake mine. He was a big enough man to take it.

"You done it, kid. Fair and square. Ain't no sense in pushin' it further. You won." My opinion of him rose considerably.

I shook his hand and said, "You're pretty good, Jack. Thanks for the games. Maybe some other time we can give it a whirl again." He agreed that might be a good idea.

All around the saloon loud conversation ensued as the crew and the townspeople fell to talking about the games. They all seemed to enjoy being together and being part of a little excitement. Then the owner walked over, and things started to settle down. When it was quiet, he spoke.

"Get the Swede." That's all he said.

Two men from town bolted out the door and were gone. I looked at Sweet, who shrugged his shoulders. From the expression on Charlie's face, it seemed he didn't know any more than we did. We had begun to work our way to the door when it suddenly opened, and the man who stood there filled the entire doorway. It was Mr. Bjornson from the general store. He was so big it seemed like the whole building tilted his way.

He made his way through the crowd to look at me. He'd obviously gotten the news that I'd beat Jack twice in less than ten minutes. Sizing me up, he seemed to find it hard to believe that the kid he was looking at could play checkers like that. Without a word he started over to the table. I looked at Charlie for help. He gave me a head sign to go on over and sit down. It was easy for him. It was *me* who had to face off with this man-mountain and play checkers!

Back at the door, people were crowding through from all over town. Somehow the word had spread in no time, and the whole town of Sweetgrass had closed up. Everyone wanted to watch some little kid from Canada take on the Swede in checkers.

The respect they showed him told me he was the presiding patriarch of checkers players in these parts, maybe in the whole northwest. That was probably supposed to mean something to me, but I didn't even have time to get scared about it.

That's when Sweet took over. He glanced over at the door and the big window fronting on the board sidewalk. The ladies and kids were stretching their necks to see, so Sweet stood up on a chair. He was going to make a speech.

"Ladies and gents, there's a lot of interest in this here contest, shared by more than just you good folks here in the saloon. I reckon it would be proper to move these proceedings to the lobby of the hotel, where ladies and kids can feel comfortable. There's a lot more room and some chairs to sit on over there. The same game rules and house rules for betting would still apply over there. The owner of this here establishment is invited to be grand marshal of the playoffs, if that suits him."

All eyes turned to the saloon owner, who pulled off his white apron and declared the saloon closed until further notice. He led the whole procession as they jammed their way out the door and hustled the few steps down to the hotel lobby.

In less than a minute they had a table and two chairs set up in the middle of the lobby, with the checkerboard and checkers in place. When the Swede sat down, his chair disappeared. The only way I knew it was still there was that every time he moved, the chair squeaked and groaned. Sitting opposite him, I knew how David in the Old Testament felt when he first looked across the creek at Goliath. Charlie quietly lifted the back brim of my hat to remind me to take it off. I handed it to Sweet.

The grand marshal made a little speech outlining the rules and told everybody to remain quiet until a game was over. Then, swelling his chest with a strong feeling for his own importance, he declared the contest begun.

The game got interesting real quick. I knew the Swede was moving too fast. I figured he underestimated me like Jack had. And sure enough, the first game lasted only fifteen moves. I could tell he knew checkers; he had just underestimated his opponent. He couldn't believe a kid had beat him.

Buzzing and talk rose all around us. When I glanced around, I could hardly believe what I saw. Every place where a human being could get, one was there. Women, kids, cowhands, the preacher, store owners—everyone who had heard about this contest was there.

The checkers were back on the black squares,and this time the Swede settled in. I could almost *feel* the power of his concentration. It was a whole different game. He took his time, moving with reasonable speed but careful to keep the position of every man in his mind at all times.

For the first time in my checkers-playing career I knew I was going to be pushed at least to the limits of my ability. I was probably going to get beat. Then some kind of an unexpected calm settled over me. It felt like everything in the world disappeared except the checkerboard. I was keeping every man in my mind, seeing the whole game at once, staying at least two moves ahead.

After about ten moves we each had six men left. He was coming up both sides while I was moving down the middle. I sacrificed a man to move my lead man to his king row, getting my first king. My strategy included stopping him from getting his first man to my king row. I knew the Swede was playing about two moves ahead, and I was watching his expression intently. I gave him another man, and he jumped. If I had calculated right, he should have known right then that he was beat.

He didn't show a sign. I gave him the second man according to my plan. He had to jump it and he did. When he put his man down and took mine off the board, he looked up at me—and I knew he knew. His last move had put the final piece of my plan in place. I moved my king, jumping three of his men. The king wound up two rows ahead of his leading man, in a position to stop him from getting the king he had to have. A little change of expression came into his eyes.

Two moves later, we each had two men left. The difference was that one of mine was that king. It was the closest game I had played in three years.

He spoke. "Py yiminy, aye tink dis poy vin dis kame."

I looked at one of the townspeople for a translation. "He thinks this boy will win this game."

Sweet made the correction. "He thinks this *man* will win the game." Smiling at Sweet, the Swede accepted the correction. He knew the game was over; there was no use playing it out. He bobbed his head at me and we smiled at each other as he reached over the table to shake my hand. When that bear paw of his closed on my hand, everything ahead of my wrist went numb. When he finally let go, I dropped my arm to my side, quietly working my fingers until I could get some feeling back into them.

The hotel lobby erupted with talk. Charlie shook my hand. Sweet handed me my hat, hugging me like a kid.

The rest of my crew started through the crowd, their hats held out. People pitched their dimes in as they passed. I believe everyone who had bet paid off without asking any questions. Even some of the women gave and collected dimes. It stopped me for a second when I saw Jack collecting dimes. He had bet on me!

The Swede got up off his chair, which looked relieved, and spoke. "Py yiminy, yew come down to my store, I giff yew dat book about da big sailing shibs. Vee talk a liddle and vee maybe play a kame in my offiss. You do dat?"

I didn't understand the "py yiminy," but I got the rest of it. "Yes sir, I would like dat." As we walked through the crowd to the door, he dropped an arm around my shoulders. It dang near knocked me to my knees, but he didn't seem to notice. I shook his hand again; he started back to his general store, and I started working the blood back into my fingers.

In the lobby, the talk centered around this youngster who had beat the best checkers player in these parts, and then it sort of mellowed into talk about just anything. I shook a lot of hands and got a lot of compliments, until finally the crowd started thinning out. Then I found Charlie and Sweet and told them I was going back to the herd.

I started down main street, but on impulse reined the sorrel around toward the general store and tied her to the hitchrack. I headed back to the Swede's "offiss," and without much in the way of preliminaries he and I were soon hunched over his own private checkerboard, going at it. He beat me the first game. We battled the second one to a draw. He guffawed and clapped me on the shoulder with that ham he was using for a hand, nearly busting my collarbone. He left the room and came back to hand me the big book about the sailing ships. I couldn't believe it.

91

After a little small talk, I figured I should be getting back to the herd. "Mr. Bjornson, I have sure enjoyed meeting you and playing checkers with you. And thank you for this book. I'll treasure it. I hope to see you again some day."

"Yew come to dis town again, yew come play checkers again, yew hear!" All totaled out, he was quite a guy. He walked with me to the front door and waved as I loped up the street and out toward the herd, working the book into my saddlebag.

When I got there, about sunset, Cookie was already starting the evening meal. He would keep the stew he made warm all evening, knowing the crew would be trickling back in until long past dark. Charlie showed up soon after I did, and we ate our meal together, laughing and talking about the day's events.

About eight we heard the sound of a freight engine followed by the rumble of empty cattle cars. They slowed, then stopped down by the loading chutes. By eleven everyone was back from Sweetgrass. Two were on first shift night duty, eight of us in our blankets. We would start before daylight.

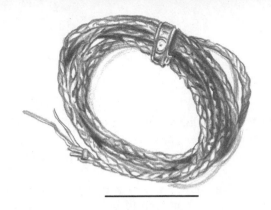

Chapter Twelve

At dawn the engine stood leaking steam in a gentle hiss. Sixty cattle cars were strung out behind it, the first three lined up with the loading chutes. We were gathered around Abraham near the cattle pens, getting our orders for loading. He was dressed in bib overalls, lace-up work shoes, a heavy buffalo robe coat, and that funny-looking hat with the ear flaps and the dangling strings.

The cars were built to hold fifty average cattle. They could be loaded and unloaded on either side, through large, heavy doors that were hung on rollers and rails so they could be rolled open and closed. The three loading chutes had been spaced to exactly match the doors into the cattle cars, so we could load three cars at a time. Abraham showed us how to open, close, and lock the big doors. We had to be careful because the railroad "couldn't be 'sponsible for no accidents." When three were loaded Abraham would signal the engineer, who would move the train forward just enough to line up the next three cars. He did it by counting the railroad ties. He knew exactly how many it took to move three car lengths.

Our job was to get the cattle up to the pens, crowding them so Abraham could move them from the pens into the alleys, up to the chutes, and into the cars. He would need one extra man on foot to open and shut the gates when Abraham said to. That way the cattle couldn't back up. Charlie pointed to Ackersley for that job.

Our assignments understood, we started toward our horses, ready to move the cattle from bedground to the pens. Abraham stopped us.

"Mistuh MacDonald suh, there is one hitch. Usually the company sends out three or four men to be sure of the count of the cattle gettin' on the train. These same men also ride in the caboose from here to Chicago, tendin' the cattle. These animals has to be unloaded for feed and water three times durin' the next five days. And 'sides that, every three or four hours someone needs to get inside the cars onto those catwalks to see that these animals is on their feet and not down gettin' hurt. To do that, these men has to walk along the tops from one cattle car to the next while the train is movin' and lower theirselves through them trap doors on the ends to get inside."

Abraham paused and we all guessed what was coming next.

"The company never had time to get four men because the telegraph lines was down. They can be heah by day aftuh tomorra if you want to wait. Otherwise some of your crew can ride with these heah critters to Chicago."

I turned my head to look at the trap doors at each end of the car and the catwalks inside. The trap doors were covered; the lids hinged on the outside edge so you could open them and lower yourself. A two-by-twelve-inch plank that ran completely around the inside of the car was high enough to be above the cattle. There was a little rail to hold onto so you wouldn't fall in with the cattle if the train swayed. If an animal was down, you had to lower yourself right in amongst them and get it back on its feet.

We realized that could be just a mite risky with a train moving about sixty miles an hour, swaying from side to side. I wondered what they paid you if you got down amongst those cows and got killed. Double wages?

"The company's willing to pay standard union wages plus meals, and you can sleep in the caboose. I suppose that might make you Great Northern Railroad employees. You might want to discuss it with your crew before we start loadin'. The company is mighty sorry and I'm sorry too, suh."

It was clear Abraham felt bad about it, but it was also clear he hadn't caused the problem. There was nobody to blame but the storm that had knocked the telegraph lines down.

We knew Charlie didn't favor waiting two extra days. The cattle were in poor enough condition as it was, and the feed out by the water tanks was about gone.

"I got to go on to Chicago anyway to handle the sale," he said, "so I'll be one of the four men. Lew has been to Chicago before, and I think he ought to come. That leaves two more. Anyone here have a mind to volunteer—knowin' we been gone sixteen days already includin' the roundup and we'll probably be gone another ten or twelve before we can get back to Raymond? We're likely needed at home right now, most of us."

I couldn't believe what I was hearing. Chicago. A day or two in Chicago! A city with all the modern things I had been reading about. I could hardly grasp hold of it in my mind.

Sweet spoke first. "I think I could make that trip without nobody at home sufferin' from my absence. I'll go."

I didn't leave any gap when he finished. "I won't be missed much, Mr. MacDonald. I'll go." I knew I sounded a little cocky, but now wasn't the time to be bashful. Charlie looked at the two of us and then his eyes worked over the rest of the crew.

"That okay with the rest of ye men?"

They voiced their agreement. I kept my eyes on Charlie and held my breath. "Okay. That's settled. We'll work out the details later. Right now we got cattle to load. Let's get to it."

My brain nearly foundered. It had all happened so fast! Me, in Chicago! Lights. Automobiles. Subways. Newspapers and magazines. Sights and sounds of a whole new modern world. At last I had a chance to see and do all the things I could only wish for and dream about in Raymond. I could hardly get my head back to the loading chutes and the herd.

We went our separate ways. Soon we were rousting the cattle off the bedground and starting them toward the alleys to the loading chutes. Charlie, Lew, and Sweet took one chute each, climbing to the top rail where they perched with a stub of a pencil and a pad to handle the all important counting jobs. We had the cattle jamming into the open gates at the north end of the pens, and Abraham set the gates on the alleys so the cattle came right on through. Real quick we found out Abraham knew two languages—American with a Southern drawl, and cow. He knew what those critters were saying to each other, and when he got down amongst them on foot they knew what he was saying. They began flowing through the alleys, up the chutes, and into the cars like a long crooked gliding snake.

The engineer leaned out the window of the engine and looked back at Abraham, waiting for his signal. When Abraham locked the last of the three doors and waved, the engineer slowly pulled the train ahead, counting the ties. As soon as the train stopped, Abraham and Ackersley opened the car doors and we started again.

We soon hit a rhythm. Before long the loading was going like clockwork. The string of loaded cars grew longer until finally there were only six empties left.

By then, all the cattle were in the alleys and the gates were locked behind them. Our work on horseback was done. We loped around to the front by the chutes to hear the final tally. We were all anxious to hear how many we had gotten through with, considering the stampede, the blizzard, and natural losses from strays wandering off unnoticed.

When we locked the door on the last car, five cars stood empty. The three men climbed down from the chutes, and Charlie added all three counts together. It tallied exactly 2,734 head. We had lost ninety-seven head. We knew fifty-seven had gone down in the stampede and that we'd lost twelve or fifteen in the blizzard. The others had simply strayed away. Some of them would probably find the home range and show up next spring.

Charlie made some calculations in his daily log, and with the count finished he now knew his original estimate was right. We were going to need eighteen dollars per head for the ones actually in the freight cars. Charlie knew enough about the Chicago market to know that eighteen would be tough, maybe impossible. He closed his log without saying anything.

"All things considered, ye did a good job, men." Charlie was smiling. We looked at each other and we were smiling too. Nothing could ever rob us of our pride in what we had done, moving those cattle through a blizzard and a stampede in the dead of the winter. We knew we had made a little history. Nobody but us and our little community of Raymond and maybe some of the people in

Sweetgrass would ever make much of it. But for us, that drive was ours as long as we lived.

Charlie got back to business. "We need to make some assignments. This is how I see it. Tommy, ye'll be responsible for gettin' the wagon and the horse herd and the crew back to Raymond. Ye'll have to take Fritz Hoffman home and tell his wife and family what happened. I'm sorry to put that off on ye, but there's nothin' else to do. Tell Mr. Baker I'll send him a telegram as soon as I've sold the cattle and have the money. Tell him I'll do the best I can fer price."

He collected his thoughts before continuing. "The four of us goin' on to Chicago will leave our mounts and saddles and gear here in Sweetgrass. Abraham can tend 'em while we're gone. Abraham says five days gettin' there, and I figure two days there closin' the sale and gettin' the money. Then two days back on a passenger train, and two days back to Raymond. So Tommy, tell our folks we'll probably show up home about twelve days from now, give or take a day or two for unexpected occurrences."

We thought that was all Charlie had to say, but his eyes swept the crew, holding us. "Likely we won't be seein' each other again as a crew. I should tell ye yer wages will be the first thing paid when I get back to Raymond, and I'm recommendin' to Mr. Baker we owe each of ye a bonus. Without takin' on undue airs, I'm thinkin' what this crew did saved us all from goin' under, back home. I know it saved David Baker. It ain't finished until we get the money in the bank, but what ye did gettin' the herd here and onto the cars is a proud thing that won't be forgotten. Ye've finished a near impossible, tough, mean job, and done it right. I'm grateful fer the respect ye've shown me and I'm proud I could be one with ye. I think that's about all, unless some of ye have somethin' to say."

No one spoke. Any more words wouldn't fit. Charlie had said it all.

"It's a little past noon. Cookie's got somethin' hot at the chuckwagon. Let's go eat and ye men can get started. Tommy, ye can still make eight miles before dark. Any questions?"

After the meal, we all made a point of shaking Cookie's hand and paying him our compliments. He stood there grinning and bowing that funny little bow from his waist, red-faced and embarrassed but feeling good because he had earned it. Then we shook hands all around, saying the little things men say instead of good-bye.

The four of us who were going to Chicago rode back to the cattle pens and put our horses in the smallest one with a water trough and feed rack. We stripped off the saddles, blankets, and bridles and walked to the little building at the corner of the pens that served as an office and living quarters for Abraham.

Abraham agreed to store our gear while we were gone and to feed and water the horses. Considering three of us were making the trip because the railroad hadn't provided its own men, he insisted he do it for free. He would even throw in two pounds of steam-rolled oats for each horse each day. He also promised me that he'd take special care of Elmer's lariat.

We took off our spurs and put them in our saddlebags, because we wouldn't need them until we got back to Sweetgrass. We left our chaps on. If we had to get down among the cattle in those cars, we wanted whatever protection they could give us.

Back out at the pens, Abraham was waiting for us. "I talked with the engineer and he knows y'all will be in the caboose. There's food and bunks there and a stove with wood and coal. Every three or four hours, check on them cattle. Be careful. Walk down the plank walkway right in the middle of the roof. There's lanterns in the caboose for nighttime work. 'Bout every thirty-six hours they'll stop at a feedyard, and the men there will unload and load 'em back up. All you got to do is be sure the same number gets on as got off. Mostly those feedyards will be plumb empty, jes like mine, so you shouldn't have no trouble. Good luck to you gennelmen. I'll be lookin' forward to seein' y'all again in about ten or twelve days."

He walked with us to the caboose. We mounted the little plat-form on the rear of it and turned to look back. Tommy was just moving the horses out with the chuckwagon. He raised a hand in a wave and we waved back. Then we opened the door of the caboose and walked inside as we heard the first rush of steam from the engine. That was followed by the blast of the whistle, and we felt a lurch as the train started its motion.

Chapter Thirteen

I was surprised at the room we had inside the caboose. There were doors at both ends with some shelves and pegs beside them for storing things and hanging clothes. Lanterns and railroad flares were stored on one of the shelves. A commode was enclosed near the rear doors. Two double bunks with blankets and pillows lined one wall. Facing the bunks a stove, with a box for firewood and coal, stood against the wall. Above it was a cupboard holding a supply of canned food, hardtack, biscuits, and crackers. There was a small counter for fixing meals, and it had drawers built into it for tin plates and cups and hardware. Next to that was a little washstand with a basin on it and a good-sized map of the United States, showing the railroads, on the wall behind it. The route of the Great Northern was marked with a heavy red line. There were a few windows along the walls and in the doors at each end, giving good light and visibility. The floor was hardwood, worn right up the middle where traffic was heaviest. The table and four chairs showed a lot of scarring and wear. The whole thing was built to be durable, not pretty.

The minute we closed the door, all four of us felt sort of cooped up. We'd been out on a limitless prairie long enough that not being able to see the sky and the skyline in all directions had us nervously looking over our shoulders.

Once we had a fire going, things warmed up. We soon took off our outer coats and chaps and hung them on the pegs. Then we washed up and sat down at the table to work out a plan. We decided each man would be responsible for fourteen cars except the one who had the cars right behind the engine. He would have thirteen. We would check them all every four hours and all go at the same time so we could help each other if something went wrong. I volunteered for the first thirteen cars and got no arguments.

For the next hour or so, we just laid in our bunks or looked out the windows at the countryside going by. It dawned on us that our worst problem for the next five days was going to be boredom. We were already starting to find out what every railroader had to deal with: doing nothing. Finally, restless, I walked over and investigated the drawers below the work counter. I found a deck of cards, a few old magazines, a dog-eared Bible, and a checkerboard. Things looked brighter with something to break the monotony.

Late that afternoon we made our first check on the cattle. My cars were the farthest up front so I went first, Sweet right behind me. I was expecting it to be pretty chancy, walking the two-foot-wide boardwalks on the tops of the cars, but to my surprise it was easy as long as I kept looking up ahead and watching for the curves. The weight of the cattle held the cars down, lessening the sway of the train. I went the full length of all sixty cars and started working back down the train.

The lock system on the trap door was simple, and I raised the door and looked in. The cattle didn't have any idea I was there. I studied them for just a minute before I lowered myself inside, grabbing the handrail when my feet settled onto the catwalk. Again I was surprised. I had figured on finding some pretty nervous critters below me, but they weren't. They were standing still, already learning to lean into the turns so they remained stable and balanced.

About the fifth or sixth car I had gotten the hang of it. I could open the doors, walk the catwalk, check the cattle, and get back out in two or three minutes. After my last car I started toward the caboose, meeting up with Sweet as he climbed out of his last car.

Back in the caboose, the four of us agreed that the assignment had sounded worse than it was. It was true, falling off the top of a car at sixty miles an hour would probably cause a guy to say a lot worse than "dang it." And having some of those animals step on you if you got mixed into them would likely cause some concern. The danger was there, but if we were careful it wouldn't be nearly as bad as it had first sounded.

Charlie got first cooking assignment and he fixed our meal that night. Cooking consisted of opening some cans, dumping the contents into a pot, and warming the pot on the stove. We had tomatoes and beef in gravy with hardtack and water. It tasted pretty good, but we all thought about Cookie as we ate it. Whatever it was he did with food, he did it right. Store-bought canned food just didn't quite cut it after eating his meals for ten days.

After supper, sitting at the table, we divided a box of matches equally among us. I shuffled the cards and dealt. Table stakes was two matches. The top limit was ten. We played blackjack for a while, then poker. I was more interested in seeing how the game went than in whether I lost or won. At first it looked like Sweet would win most of the matches, but two hours later it had pretty well evened out again. Taking gambles was part of everyday life for a cowhand. I think that's why every one of them I ever knew thought he was a pretty good poker player. After the card game we took the lanterns and checked the cattle again.

By noon the next day we had settled into a routine. In our free time we studied the big map and were soon interested in the new country we were seeing. We could track where we were by the signs we passed once in a while. We followed the Milk River until it joined the Yellowstone and the Missouri right at the border of Montana and North Dakota. We ran within seeing distance of the Missouri for a long ways. We crossed the river twice on bridges, but the train never did come very close to any large towns.

That afternoon, the train stopped at a place the map didn't show. As soon as we quit rolling, a crew of men started to unload the cattle. We went out to watch and help if we could, but they had a system and could probably do it better without us. They knew their business; it only took a little over an hour to empty all fifty-five cars. After the cattle had filled on hay, grain, and water, we counted them back into the cars as the yard crew reloaded them. The count came out exactly right.

At Minot, North Dakota, the train slowed while they switched us to the south fork of the Great Northern. For a long time after that turn, we ran on wide-open prairie without seeing a single house or town. At the Minnesota border we were again switched. Holding to the south fork of the Great Northern, we crossed the Red River of the North. After we passed through the outskirts of Moorhead, Minnesota, we angled back south again.

The third day, after the midday cattle check, I climbed down over the coal car to the engine and knocked. A surprised engineer opened the door. I asked him if I could watch him run the train and, glad to have company, he invited me in. After that I spent my spare time with him, learning the routine of making a steam engine run. When the engineer saw how it fascinated me, he let me handle the throttle and the brakes when no towns were in sight, watching to be sure I did it right. Sweet got interested too, and after he learned the fundamentals we took turns handling the controls.

The cattle were fed and watered just after we left Fargo, at Moorhead, and once more in Wisconsin at a place without a town in sight. Each time, the crews did a good job of getting the cattle off, fed, and back on, and the count continued to be right. While the cars were empty they opened drains in the floors and turned large pressure hoses of water to the task of washing all the manure out. They let the floors dry for a while, then closed the drains and threw a little clean sand around the cars to give the cattle solid footing. We felt useless and nervous watching someone else handle our cattle, like we were shirking our duty.

Late in the afternoon of the fourth day, the engineer said we'd be pulling into the Chicago stockyards about seven the next morning. I remember the shiver that ran through me as I thought about it. Sometime in the night we crossed from Wisconsin into Illinois. After our two-o'clock check that morning, I couldn't go back to sleep. I saw a sign that said "Elgin" as we slowed and then regained our speed; on the map that town wasn't far from Chicago.

In the dark just preceding dawn I felt the train begin to slow. I dressed quickly and sat by the window watching the lights pass. We were rolling slowly through a continuous string of towns, which I finally realized were the suburbs leading into Chicago. In the last few miles of that trip, I saw more towns and more people than I had seen in my whole life back in Raymond. I wondered what the switchyards and the stockyards would look like.

Chapter Fourteen

The train crept the last couple of miles into the switchyard. I went to the little platform at the rear of the caboose and leaned around, straining to see ahead. The world had suddenly become a mass of railroad tracks, running generally parallel but angling in and out in a crisscross pattern that seemed endless. Engines puffed and strained everywhere, blowing steam, sounding whistles, ringing bells, some with no cars, some with a few, one with a string so long I couldn't see the end of it.

Everything was black and dirty. The ground was dark with soot, the railroad ties black with creosote. The rails were black except on top, where they were shiny from use. Men dressed in soot-covered overalls moved busily, calling orders, checking rails, waving to engineers and each other. The outer edge of the switchyard was more than a half mile away on either side. I couldn't imagine how anyone could ever keep all those trains on the right tracks and going the right direction.

We felt our train move to our right, south, as it came through about four or five switches. We slowly cleared the center of the yard and then picked up just a little speed. I thought we would move right into the stockyards, but after about ten more minutes we slowed again, jerking farther south as we passed through two more switches.

Still leaning over the rail of the caboose, looking forward, I finally saw the heavy fence on the west side of the stockyards, maybe half a mile ahead. The fence ran south, to my right, out of sight.

Even in the still, cold air, a stench lay like an invisible oppressive cloud. The smell of livestock was part of my life, but this was different—five hundred thousand tons of manure and urine that had accumulated over several years from millions of cattle and hogs and sheep and horses, exposed to summer heat and winter wet and growing ever more stagnant and putrid. I could handle it, but it was the strongest animal smell I had ever been close to. I didn't even want to think what it would be like just after the spring rains came and the weather warmed up.

The tracks we were on ran along the north edge of the stockyards past the unloading chutes. As we approached, I climbed the ladder onto the top of the caboose and stood there absolutely thunderstruck at the vastness of the stockyards. They stretched off straight ahead almost out of sight, and probably more than a mile to my right. Including the streets, parking lots, and surrounding roads, these yards covered more than a whole section of land, a lot more than a square mile. The alleys for moving the cattle in and out divided the yard into strips. Between the alleys were pens of all sizes and shapes, reminding me of a gigantic, intricate patchwork quilt. There had to be six or eight thousand pens. Even in the dead of the winter, out of the livestock season, there were so many cattle and hogs and sheep in them I couldn't guess the number. There must have been eighty or a hundred thousand, maybe more.

Steam was rising from the water troughs where water was running and from fifty thousand fresh manure droppings. Vapor was coming out the muzzle of every animal there. Men bundled up against the cold and wearing rubber boots were moving cattle from one pen to another, checking written orders as they set the gates to make the moves. There was a never-ending roar of bawling, whinnying, bleating, and braying. I must have stood for two or three full minutes taking in the huge and unreal scene.

The cold brought me back to reality and I looked around to see where Chicago was. North, less than five miles away, I could make out the shapes of tall, square buildings in the morning smoke and haze.

Forcing myself back off the roof of the caboose, I went down to the other men to get ready for the unloading. As far as I knew, we would count the cattle off the cars into one big pen. After they were unloaded an agent representing the buyer would have a look at them to determine their quality. We would take his written order to Billy Daniels, the buyer. Daniels would work out a price with Charlie. It sounded simple.

The stockyards were bounded on the north by Exchange Avenue and on the west by Halsted. The tracks came in between Exchange and the chutes. Between the tracks and Exchange were some buildings that served as offices for stockyard business. As we pulled in, two men came out of an office building and walked over to the unloading chutes. They were wearing white shirts, ties, and felt dress hats. Zipper galoshes protected their Oxford shoes from the mud and manure of the loading chutes and cattle pens. Their outer coats were made of some kind of slick, pretty material. They walked up to the man in charge of assigning incoming cattle to pens and handed him a written order.

Once off the train, Charlie introduced us and we shook hands all around. The agent, Duane Carlson, seemed like a pretty decent guy. He explained that he wanted to walk through the cattle to estimate weight and quality so he could make up a work order for Billy Daniels. The stockyard man in charge of the pens asked who would be responsible for the cattle, and Charlie said he would until they were bought by Daniels. The man asked if Charlie had money to pay the usual daily rate if the cattle didn't sell. Charlie said he had it, or could arrange it; when he mentioned the Baker ranch in Alberta the man seemed satisfied. He started back to give orders to the unloading crew while Carlson and the other man came with us to the chutes.

The stockyard crew soon had the locks open and the first five cars unloaded. The five unloading chutes emptied into one large alley that led to a huge pen with a feed manger down one side and water troughs at both ends. We stood on one side of the gate and Carlson and his friend stood on the other to make our counts.

We all counted 2,734 head, and Charlie relaxed a little. Too

105

many times in other cattle deals he had been forced to make a second count on horseback when the buyers somehow came up eight or ten short.

I took a look at Lew and Sweet as we watched the yardmen close the gates on the pen. We had delivered the herd to the end of the line. We still had to set a price, get the money, and take it back to Raymond—but having those cattle safe in the pen at the Chicago stockyard felt awful good.

Carlson, who had made some notes on a pad of paper, gave us a head signal to follow him. We left the pens and crossed the tracks to the office building. As we walked, Carlson said he figured the cattle were in pretty poor shape. He could still use them, but they would have to be bought as cutter or canner grade, which meant a low price. He figured they would dress out somewhere near forty-six or forty-seven percent, considering they were pretty skinny with a lot of bone and hide compared to the meat. The final price, he said, was up to Billy Daniels. Charlie didn't commit his ideas one way or the other.

In the office building, Carlson took us into a room marked GREAT NORTHERN LAND AND CATTLE. He invited us to sit down while he made out the work order we would take to Daniels. We had about three or four minutes to wait. The others in the office were busy with adding machines, telephones, and ledgers. But I was aware they looked us over more than once in that short amount of time.

On the way out, work order in hand, Charlie stopped at the big office in the center of the building. The latest price quotations and sales volumes for all kinds of livestock and feed were posted on an enormous blackboard that took up one whole wall. Phones were ringing all over the place, with dozens of conversations going on at once. One man was in motion the whole time we were there, erasing and changing numbers according to the latest news from all over the country that was coming in by telephone. This was the nerve center of the livestock business in midwestern America.

According to the big blackboard, cutter and canner grade cattle were only drawing between $15.00 and $17.50 per head. My heart sank. We weren't going to get what we needed. I glanced at Charlie; his only reaction was to flex his jaw muscles once and keep reading. Utility grade cattle were drawing between $18.00 and $19.00 per head, average. Charlie made a couple of entries in his daily log, and then we walked out front to wait for the taxicab that would take us to Billy Daniels.

Chapter Fifteen

While we waited for the taxi, we took off our chaps and draped them over our shoulders. There was a look of wonderment on the driver's face when he pulled up and saw our trail clothes. Charlie told him Daniels' address—Drexel Arms Hotel—and got into the front seat. The rest of us crowded into the back and the driver started the cab moving, working with the gearshift that was anchored in the floorboards.

My eyes were wide as we drove to a main road and turned north toward the Chicago skyline. The road had two lanes of traffic in each direction, and I saw more automobiles in ten minutes than I had seen in my whole life. We drove past every kind of store the mind of man can think of. Grocery stores, drug stores, dry goods, hardware, bars, hotels, cafes, offices, junkyards, schoolyards, fenced-in yards we couldn't see into, buildings going up and buildings being torn down. Pretty soon I couldn't see any more grass or trees, just cement or brick or asphalt.

People on the sidewalks were dressed in a lot of different ways, but most of them wore work clothes and work shoes, with caps instead of hats on their head. Delivery trucks were everywhere—meat wagons, milk trucks, bakery trucks, fruit and vegetable trucks, buses, dry goods trucks, furniture trucks. Most of them had big signs painted on their sides with all kinds of pictures and words to get your attention.

As we got closer to downtown Chicago I could hardly believe what I began to see on the buildings. More signs. All kinds of signs. Signs in lights and in long tubes of glass that formed writing; painted signs, picture signs, written signs, signs everywhere.

The driver turned onto a street named Union Boulevard, stopped about a block later, and pointed out the Drexel Arms Hotel. We got out, our chaps still draped over our shoulders, and Charlie paid our fare. Lew led the way. He and Charlie had both been in Chicago before, so they had some kind of feeling for what we were getting into.

I dang near died when I saw the front door of the hotel. It was four glass doors joined together on one edge. You went through it while it was turning. Lew and Charlie went first, and I watched carefully to see how it was done. Timing was important, and when it was lined up just right, I stepped into it while it was still moving. I got through okay and looked back to see that Sweet had made it too. I wondered what you did if you changed your mind or made a misstep getting into it. Heavy as it was, that thing would probably break a few ribs if you made a mistake. I figured that door was just one step ahead of pure dumb.

Having survived the door, I turned to size up the lobby. For the first time in my life my jaw dropped clear down to my belt buckle. I had never heard of, or even seen a picture of, anything so plush and fancy. The light fixture that hung from the high ceiling must have cost as much as the whole town of Raymond. That thing was at least twelve feet across with about a thousand little light bulbs all over it. Some were hidden by strings of cut glass that made loops and circles in beautiful designs.

The floor was covered with deep red carpet, and a man was constantly moving about with a dustpan and brush, keeping it spotless. I got the feeling the carpet was made to look at, not walk on.

There must have been fifteen big mirrors on the walls along with six or eight great big paintings of mountain scenes and oceans and such. Burnished brass light fixtures with lightbulbs and shades hung on the walls. I felt like I was in a huge, colorful, well-lit cavern.

The smell in the lobby made my nose wrinkle. It seemed like

a mixture of soap, cleaning compound, and real sweet pipe to-bacco. It wasn't objectionable, just strong.

Charlie shifted his chaps from his shoulder to his arm, carrying them low to keep from drawing attention. Each of us did the same. We stepped up to the registration desk, which had a sign that said INFORMATION. Another sign. It seemed like nobody in Chicago would know where to go for anything without a sign. The desk was made of dark, polished wood with hand-carved figures along the front. It was so fancy and shiny I was afraid to touch it. The clerk on duty looked at us once, then ran his eyes over us again— the same thing that the Great Northern office workers, the taxi driver, and the hotel doorman had done. I was getting a little tired of being looked at like I was some sort of a circus freak, so I took a little step forward and made it pretty obvious I was giving this clerk the once-over, too.

He was dressed in a suit that pinched him in the shoulders, a white shirt, and a celluloid collar with a tie that was off center. His hair was greased and parted in the middle, and by the way he carried his nose a little too high and kept looking down it, I figured he was a great big zero hiding behind a desk and acting snooty just to keep anyone from figuring him for what he was. I did my level best to tell him all that with the look on my face.

Sweet was fighting to hold back a grin. I knew what was going through his mind. This officious little clerk would last about ten seconds at six o'clock in the morning on horseback on the dark prairie, forty degrees below zero in a thirty-mile-an-hour wind, with twenty-eight hundred head of cattle about to stampede for two miles.

"We are supposed to meet a Mr. Billy Daniels here. Could ye tell me where I might find him?" Charlie asked.

From the expression on the clerk's face when he answered, I figured he had gas from a bad breakfast. "Mr. Daniels is upstairs, second floor, room 210."

We started toward the great big staircase off to the right. It was carpeted all the way up, with beautiful hand-carved banisters on both sides. Behind us, the dustpan man swept up little crumbs of dried manure that had fallen from our boots onto his beloved carpet. I had nothing against him, but I felt glad somehow that I had left a little manure on the carpet.

In the hallway, just before we arrived at room 210, Charlie stopped. "I did some figurin'. We got to have at least eighteen a head to come out on this deal. Cutter and canner cattle ain't goin' to draw that on today's market." He didn't say any more. He didn't have to. Had we come all this way to make a losing deal?

Charlie knocked on the door, and a man opened it and invited us in. Just inside was a waiting room with a desk and chairs and a davenport for visitors. The man opened another door into an office and told Billy Daniels we were there.

After introductions and handshakes all around, I realized Billy Daniels hadn't always been in an office. His handshake was hard and firm. When I looked in his face, I saw the crow tracks coming from the outer corners of his eyes. I could tell he'd spent some time sitting around campfires and working cattle from a horse. We all took seats—Charlie opposite Daniels' desk, the rest of us on chairs close to a wall. Charlie handed Carlson's work sheet over, and Daniels studied it carefully. Then he raised his eyes, looking shrewd.

"Looks like we got some cutter and canner beef here. Not much market for them right now. Price is depressed. Maybe we can use 'em and maybe we can't. Maybe I can take 'em off your hands."

He was wasting no time. We were into the heart of our whole gamble in bringing the beef to Chicago almost without time to get warmed up for it. None of us moved a muscle. We acted like that's just what we expected to hear while we waited for Charlie's response.

Charlie looked disinterested and shifted in his chair like he was going to get up. "Well, we thought we'd give ye first chance to offer. Don't want to take yer time if it's a burden on ye."

Daniels picked it up. "I suppose I owe it to you men to at least make an offer. I think I can take the cattle, straight through, fifteen dollars a head."

My heart sank. At that price or even close to it, most of the folks at home were out of business.

"That's cutter and canner and junk animal prices." Charlie sounded a little offended. "These animals are all at least utility. Quotations this mornin' were above nineteen on some of 'em. Last year's average price fer all cattle going through the stockyards was $23.38 a head—except milk cows; they was about thirty.

There wasn't a quote on the boards this mornin' for anything walkin' less than seventeen dollars. Fifteen doesn't even come close. Thanks fer yer time, Mr. Daniels."

Daniels was surprised when Charlie came right back at him like that. It was becoming plain to me that these two old warriors were going head to head on what was shaping up to be a real dicker. Talk about playing poker! We were playing this game called bluff for folks who would fold if we didn't win.

Daniels snorted. "Sixteen dollars. Tops." Charlie came right back at him. "Nineteen seventy-five, bottom dollar."

Daniels poked his finger at his work sheet. "The work sheet says they won't dress better than forty-five percent." Charlie looked disgusted. "Your work sheet says about forty-six or forty-seven percent," he corrected. "My work sheet says the whole herd will average forty-eight, dressed and on the hook. Maybe forty-nine."

A rap on the door interrupted us.

The man from the outer office stuck his head in, and Daniels motioned him over. We could overhear their conversation. Daniels' daughter, Phyllis, was outside wanting to see her father. Daniels said to tell her he'd be with us for a few more minutes. Then he got back to business.

"None of those animals can be put into the feed pens and fattened. Too far gone and not thrifty. Right now their hipbones and ribs are nearly sticking through the hide. A lot of them are going to go for canners. Anything above seventeen fifty is out of the question." He waited for Charlie's answer.

"These animals is all young heifers and steers. There ain't an old hard-boned shelly cow among 'em, and we'll guarantee none of 'em will grade cutter or canner. On that basis, nineteen dollars," Charlie said firmly.

"Fifteen dollars for every animal that grades cutter or canner, seventeen fifty for all the rest. Slaughterhouse to determine grade."

Another rap sounded at the door. Phyllis wanted to see dad. Daniels got irritated. "Tell Phyllis to sit down and wait. I'm real busy for a few minutes."

Charlie came back at Daniels. "Fifteen dollars for every animal that grades canner. Nineteen fifty for all the rest. U.S government to determine grade."

"Aw, we're getting too complicated. Seventeen fifty straight through. No more offers." Daniels looked determined and Charlie looked offended.

Charlie continued. "Nineteen twenty-five straight through. No more offers."

Another rap at the door. The man outside stuck his head in again and it was plain to see that he hated what was about to happen. Phyllis was going to see dad, or else.

"Tell that girl to sit down and wait! I can't be interrupted right now. I'll be finished in about ten minutes." The door closed.

"Where will you find another buyer if I don't take them?"

This time there was no rap. The door opened and in walked Phyllis. All of us stood except Daniels, and I got my first look at her. I darn near fell back into my chair.

Phyllis was all ages between thirteen and twenty-five, depending on what part of her you were looking at. I estimated she had been born about nineteen years ago. With all the paint she was wearing on her face she looked about twenty-five. From the look of the sleeveless white satin dress she was nearly wearing, cut low both front and back, she looked about sixteen. Her beaded white headband made her look like a kid fourteen playing dress-up. From her manners, she was a spoiled rotten thirteen-year-old. I'd seen squaws on the Blood Indian reservation back home wearing paint and a beaded headband like that, but that was during a rain dance at their fall celebration. Her shoes were just a bunch of imitation leather straps with a skinny heel and nothing else. Over her arm she carried a white coat with a fur collar.

She walked past like she didn't see us right up to Daniels' desk. "Daddy, I need the keys to your car."

"Not now, Phyllis. Wait in the foyer while I finish with these men."

She didn't even glance at us. "These men won't mind the interruption, daddy. Can't I just take the keys and go?"

"I want to talk to you about the car before you take it. Go out and wait just a few minutes."

He was getting pretty firm. She was getting pretty irritated. I was getting pretty educated.

She turned and looked at us like we were interfering with her—like she was a whole lot more important than working out a price for cattle we had just spent three weeks moving halfway across the continent, getting a man killed in the process.

We didn't have long to wait to see what was so all-fired important about her getting his keys right now. "Daddy, it won't wait. Jason will be in the lobby in about two minutes, and we want to leave as soon as he gets here. My car won't carry the four of us, so I'll leave it for you. I'll need your sedan. Give me the keys."

Daniels looked like he was struggling to keep from turning her over his knee. "Phyllis, I don't want you going out with that Jason any more. He's a worthless playboy. And you aren't driving forty miles just for a dance. Now sit down in the foyer and wait! I'll be done pretty soon and we can talk it over."

Phyllis suddenly became coy and sickening. "Now, daddy. We aren't kids. Please don't make this worse than it needs to be. I'm sure you don't want to embarrass these . . . gentlemen . . . any more than you have."

She turned to look at us. She probably meant to act real cute and charming, but I can hardly describe the expression that crossed her face for a split second. If we'd been four gorillas standing there, she couldn't have looked more disgusted.

I suppose the four of us didn't look like real winners. We had our big wide-brimmed hats in our hands and were wearing our riding boots. Our outer coats were walking billboards of the trail drive and the meals we'd eaten at campfires. Our scarves were wrapped high around our necks, and we had our gloves on. None of us had shaved for a few days. I know we smelled of smoke and sweat and manure.

But even giving her the benefit of the doubt about all that, there was still no excuse for her barging in like she did, assuming her afternoon dance was more important than us trying to keep fifty ranchers afloat. I'd never seen anyone so selfish and disagreeable. No kid back home would ever dare to talk back to his folks that way.

Daniels jammed his hand in his pocket and tossed out a ring of keys. Phyllis picked them up, smiled sweetly, and thanked him. Before she left she glanced again at the four of us like we had crawled out of a badger hole.

115

I shot a look at Sweet. His eyes mirrored mine. His face looked like he had a belly ache. We wrote Phyllis off, turning our attention back to Charlie.

It was quiet while Daniels looked at his work order and then at some notes he'd made, struggling to recover from the rage he felt at being trapped and humiliated by his daughter. Finally he was ready to get back to the dicker.

"Eighteen dollars. Take it or leave it."

"We'll leave it. Thanks fer your time." That was the figure we were after! What was wrong with Charlie? We were all careful not to let our surprise show—but inside I was really worried that Charlie had held out too long for too high a price. Then I relaxed. Charlie knew what he was doing.

Charlie stood, so we all stood with him, and I took a step toward the door. Running a bluff sometimes takes a little help.

"That your last word?" Daniels looked up at us, his face smug.

Charlie answered in real short, clipped words. "No. My last word is eighteen seventy-five, straight through." He was on his way to the door as he spoke.

I was turning the knob when Daniels stood. "You're doing me dirty but I'll pay it. I shouldn't, but I will. I'll lose money as sure as I'm sitting here." He was acting pained, like we'd done him wrong. Charlie turned back to him, and the two reached out to shake hands. At that moment their entire demeanors changed. Their handshake was genuine; they were both satisfied! Poker can't compare to the gambling done by two experienced cattlemen who get together to buy and sell.

The handshake was all they required. They didn't need it in writing. I made some quick calculations and realized that Charlie had gotten just over fifty-one thousand dollars for the cattle—more money than we'd hoped for, more than I'd ever dreamed of. Sweet was holding on to keep from letting out a rebel yell.

"How do you want your money?" Daniels asked Charlie.

"Bank cashier's check all right?" Charlie answered.

"I'll have one ready for you day after tomorrow at this office by three o'clock. Who do I make it out to?"

"Baker Ranch, In Trust. Can I get about five hundred of it in cash fer some expenses and the trip back?"

"Sure. Have much trouble moving those animals?" With the dicker behind them, Daniels was a real friendly, easygoing guy.

Charlie looked at us and a funny kind of smile tugged at the corners of his mouth. "A little. We had a blizzard and lost a man in a run one mornin'." Daniels stopped still. I knew he felt the loss of Fritz even though he didn't know him or know exactly how it happened. I was more sure than ever that he'd been on trail drives before. This man was all right. I felt a sense of kinship with him and sympathy for his problem with his daughter.

"When you come for the check, plan to spend a minute. I want to hear some of the details. I've been stuck here in this office, in this city, too long." His eyes looked wistful for a minute, and I figured he was thinking about Phyllis, trying to work out what had gone wrong. If he'd been raised out on some ranch somewhere, as I suspected, and had moved to the city because he thought it had advantages, I could understand what he was feeling, seeing that Phyllis had turned out the way she had.

I got just that far when the shock of what I was thinking set into my system. Something was real wrong here. I had been thinking that getting out of Raymond to a city would be a great big, thrilling, unbelievable adventure. A modern city was supposed to make a guy into a gentleman, able to move up in the world and to get all the things that make life worthwhile.

And Daniels had done exactly that. He'd left the country and was in Chicago with cars and a fancy hotel office, making big cattle deals. And yet he was talking about his need to get out of the city and back to a town about like Raymond!

And what had gone wrong with Phyllis? With every advantage in her favor, money and city life and cars and friends, how did she turn out to be the most thoughtless, rude, empty-headed excuse for a human being I had ever seen?

I thought about mother—the clothes and money and advantages she'd never had, the tough life that was the only life she knew. And I realized mother was fifty times the woman Phyllis Daniels was ever going to be! That about knocked me over, because I'd never thought of mother that way.

All this started to get mixed up with the confusion I'd felt when I rode away from home in the freezing darkness more than two weeks ago. When I rode out, it was pretty clear to me that Jacob and Elmer just didn't understand how things were, and they probably never would. Not as long as they stayed in Raymond, thinking the same thoughts, accepting the poverty, just living to die. Now here was Daniels, with everything that was supposed to cure our problems at home. Yet he was cornered, getting beat up by his daughter, facing the near certainty she would break his heart. Between the two of us, I didn't know who had it worse—us up there, or Daniels down here.

Where was the sense to all this? Why did this whole thing turn out backwards?

I realized Charlie had been looking at me, and he must have been reading some of the thoughts on my face. He held his peace, though. I found out later he was just waiting for the right time.

We had started down the hall when we heard the door open behind us. Daniels came out and called to Charlie. "You got rooms in some other hotel?"

"No. We were just going to the lobby to make a plan."

"Tell you what. You set aside a little time to have dinner with me tomorrow night here in the hotel restaurant, and I'll arrange rooms for you here and pay the bill. But I won't do it for free. I want to talk with you about the cattle business up around Cardston. I think you can give me some ideas and information I need. You're going to tell me about that drive, too. Is it a deal?"

Charlie looked at us and we agreed. "Deal," Charlie answered. Daniels might want some information, but more than that, I figured, he wanted us to share the drive with him.

Daniels came down to the registration desk and we arranged for rooms for each of us. The clerk wasn't quite so uppity this time, although I did see his nose wrinkle once or twice as he caught the smell of campfires and sweat coming from our clothes.

Before we separated to go to our rooms, Lew stopped us. Giving direct compliments wasn't something our kind did very often, but Lew did it this time. "Charlie, I intend makin' it known back home that you are responsible for savin' most of the ranchers. Gettin' the cattle here was somethin' shared by all of us, but playin' the game with Daniels was just you. Speakin' for us all, thanks."

Lew put out his hand and the two shook hands. Sweet and I spoke our thanks along with Lew. Charlie looked a little embarrassed and mumbled something about that dicker not amounting to much. Not amount to much? The whole south end of the Province of Alberta had hung in the balance for the minutes it took Charlie to outbluff Daniels.

We turned to the business at hand—looking on our keys for our room numbers. Mine was number 245, next to Lew's, number 247. Sweet and Charlie were across the hall, 246 and 248.

I turned the key in the lock and swung the door open.

Chapter Sixteen

I stepped in and stopped dead in my tracks. I had never seen a room so splendid. The floor was covered with a deep wine-colored carpet, the walls with a light-colored, wine-striped wallpaper. Against one wall was a neatly made brass bed. In one corner was a built-in desk with a chair, writing tablet, and lamp. In the opposite corner, a full-length mirror on the front of it, was a door leading to a closet for hanging clothes. The light fixtures were beautifully crafted, shiny brass. There were a couple of stuffed chairs covered with fabric.

With my eyes still wide in wonder, I walked across the room to open another door and discovered the bathroom. I had never seen indoor plumbing or an indoor bathtub in my life. It was all so shiny and white and sanitary looking I just stood there in amazement. Then I tried to figure out what each of the fixtures was supposed to do.

I knew what the washbasin was for, and I was pretty sure about the bathtub. I figured out what the toilet was for, but I couldn't tell how it worked. It was full of water and bolted to the floor. After you used it, how did you dump it? I'd have to ask Lew or Charlie.

I was also having trouble figuring out the bathtub. It was built into a little cove with a two-part glass door, half of which would slide back and forth. I figured maybe it was so if a guy wanted privacy he could just close it.

By the washbasin was a rack filled with the thickest, fluffiest towels and washcloths I had ever seen. They felt so good I had to stand there and touch them for a while. Then I went and sat in one of the chairs and just gazed around at the most luxurious, beautiful bedroom and bathroom I had ever seen. A rap at the door brought me back to reality. It was Charlie.

"We figure on goin' up the street; we'll be needing some clothes and things. There's an Emporium three or four blocks from here. Better come along, Henry."

They didn't have to ask twice. I couldn't wait to get out to look at Chicago. I didn't know what an Emporium was, but I had to start somewhere. Charlie and Lew took the lead, Sweet and I following. Walking up the street I got a chance to look in some of the windows. It was a wonder to me how many different kinds of goods were for sale in those four blocks.

I had never seen traffic to compare with the amount on these streets. Automobiles, buses, and trucks of every description honked and turned and ground their gears. Streetcars on fixed tracks clanged back and forth. There was even a train whizzing along on a trestle fifteen feet above street level that stopped to let people off and on. I also saw an odd-shaped structure rising from the sidewalk with a broad staircase that went down into the ground. Above it was a sign that said SUBWAY. I'd read about them, but I'd never seen one.

At every corner we had to stop and wait for a light to tell us when to go and when to stop for the unending stream of cars. I had to wrinkle my nose at the smell of burned automobile gasoline.

Four blocks down, Lew glanced up and my eyes followed his to a building that was three stories high with a six-foot-wide sign on it that said EMPORIUM. We pushed through the big door and stopped for a minute trying to get our wits about us. We could see no end to the counters and racks, all crowded with every kind of thing that could be sold. There were signs everywhere. There must have been two hundred people shopping on that one floor.

Lew located a round desk not far from the doors with a big sign on it that said INFORMATION. Following directions, we soon found ourselves in the midst of enough trousers, shirts, socks, coats, hats, shoes, underwear, belts, and boots to outfit all the men in Calgary, maybe in all of Alberta. A man walked up and asked if he could help us find something.

Soon we had new trousers, shirts, low-cut Oxford shoes, socks, good coats, and long-handled cotton underwear. We also picked out things to shave and clean up with. There were cash registers everywhere; we picked the nearest one and settled up.

It was just beginning to get dark when we got back to the hotel. As I opened the door to my room, I said to Lew, "I figured out what the toilet was, but I don't know how to empty it. How do I do it?"

"Look behind and above it on the wall. There's a water tank up there with a chain and a handle hanging down. Just pull on the handle and it will flush out the toilet with water."

"What about the bathtub? What's the business with the glass door?"

"That's so you can close it and take a shower instead of a bath."

I'd never even heard of a shower. "How do I work the shower?"

"Look at the fixtures that operate the tub. The one in the middle's for the shower. Turn on the tap to the tub and pull that button up, and the water will come out of a nozzle above your head. Keep the tub unplugged and it will just keep running as long as you want to stand there."

I was dumbfounded at the thought of it. I couldn't imagine what it would feel like and couldn't wait to find out. As I unlocked my door, Charlie spoke up. "In about an hour a man will come to yer door. Give him yer old clothes and he'll get them cleaned. Give him yer boots, too. He'll return them in the mornin'." I couldn't believe it. One amazing thing after another.

In my room, I unwrapped my new clothes and laid them on the bed. Then I peeled off my old ones down to my long-handled underwear and walked into the bathroom.

Before actually getting into the bathtub, I studied the water fixtures until I was sure what each one was for. I turned on the hot and cold water until the temperature was right, then I pulled up the stem that said SHOWER. The full load of water came out of a nozzle above me and hit me in the back of the head. I had to laugh in spite of the wet surprise. Maybe it should have said PULL AND JUMP BACK.

I tugged off my long-handles, stepped in, and closed the sliding half of the glass door. I probably stayed in there for forty-five

123

minutes, soaping and resoaping the thick cloth, washing and scrubbing, sometimes just standing and letting the water cascade over me. I couldn't believe this kind of luxury existed. I don't think I had been so clean since the day I was born.

When I finally got out, the room was filled with steam, so I opened the door to let it clear while I dried off in a huge, soft, thick towel. I put on my new long-handles, shaved what fuzz I had, and got into my new clothes. The trousers were stiff with newness and the Oxford shoes had an unfamiliar feeling. I gathered up my old clothes and boots and lay them by the door. Sure enough, a minute or two later a man came and took them away.

When he left, I went into the bathroom to go to the toilet. After I finished I worked patiently to get the paper off the roll. Then I stood to examine the water tank and chain on the wall above me.

I had no idea what would happen when I pulled the handle on the chain. For just a minute I figured I had turned the Missouri River loose. The sound of water crashing down out of the tank into the toilet froze me in my tracks. The toilet filled immediately, swirling so high I knew it would come right over the edge. I took a step back, ready to run for Lew, certain I had broken it.

Then, almost as quickly as it started, the water stopped rushing and settled down, and the toilet looked just like it did before I sat down.

Gingerly I reached up and pulled the chain again. This time I didn't flinch, but I was still a little unnerved. That had to be the cleverest idea ever invented. A toilet that could fire and reload, totally automatic. Looking behind me to be sure I was still alone, I fired it once more. I walked out of the bathroom feeling pretty smart and sophisticated.

I gave it a few more minutes before I walked to Sweet's room. Our stomachs said it was supper time, and soon the four of us were headed to the hotel restaurant.

A man wearing a white shirt, bow tie, and red vest came over, a towel draped over his arm. He left us four big fold-open menus, in which I got lost in no time at all.

Lew ordered for all of us. We had soup, prime rib roast with baked potatoes, and string beans on the side, followed by a piece of pie. That was the fanciest, tastiest meal I'd ever seen or eaten.

It was close to eight o'clock when we finished. Charlie and Lew figured they would step into another section of the hotel to watch a man play a piano while a woman sang. I didn't have much desire for that, nor did Sweet. I suggested we take a little walk to see the lights at night. Charlie said to be careful as we walked out onto Union Boulevard.

Everywhere we looked were lights—big and small, some constant, others flashing on and off. Because we were dressed in our new clothes, no one paid us very much attention. We both felt half naked without out hats. I had never realized how much a hat can become part of you when you've worn it most of your life.

Sweet and I walked quite a distance and then worked our way back to the hotel. Charlie and Lew weren't in the lobby or the parlor, so we figured they'd gone to bed. We rode the elevator up to the second floor, said good-night, and went into our rooms.

I hung my new coat in the closet and sat down for a few minutes. Then on an impulse, I opened my door a crack to look out. No one was there, so I went back down the hall to the elevator. I rode it clear to the twelfth floor, walked quickly to the end of the hall, and pushed the curtain aside. I stood there gazing down at Union Boulevard for probably ten or fifteen minutes, watching the lights, the automobiles, and the people moving up and down. It was a sight I don't think I'll ever forget.

I rode the elevator back down to the lobby, then back up to the second floor. Getting from one floor to another without doing all the work myself was just too much fun to pass up.

Back to my room, I still wasn't ready for bed, so I pulled off my clothes and took another hot shower. Half an hour later I dried off and got back into my new long-handles, feeling warm and drowsy.

I carefully pulled down the bedspread. On the bed were two of the whitest pillows I had ever seen. I slipped underneath the sheet and blanket and turned the lamp light off. I knew it was the best bed I had ever slept in. All my muscles and my mind started to relax. As I drifted off, I was seeing lights and signs and automobiles everywhere, and then a spoiled girl in a white dress who needed a good licking, and finally Union Boulevard twelve stories below.

Chapter Seventeen

I stood in the shower a long time after rolling out of bed, not because I needed it but because I still couldn't believe the luxury. It wasn't quite time for breakfast yet, so while I waited I flushed the toilet a time or two and watched it work.

We had bacon, eggs, and toast for breakfast. Lew also ordered us four big glasses of fresh-squeezed orange juice. I'd eaten a few oranges at Christmas time up home, but I'd never tasted the fresh-squeezed juice. I don't think I'd ever tasted anything that surprised me so with its sweetness. I drank it real slow, aware the others were smiling, taking pleasure in my enjoyment.

As we left the restaurant Lew asked if any of us had anything special in mind. The day was open until six, when we were to meet Billy Daniels for supper. When we shook our heads no, Lew said, "I think we all might do with a visit to the barber." A moment of looking at each other and then at the others in the lobby told us he was right.

The hotel barber shop was fascinating, with all kinds of bottles of tonics and two big basins that were used for giving shampoos. The padded leather barber chairs had foot pedals and went up and down when the pedals were pumped. The barbers, dressed in white knee-length dusters, looked very auspicious. They were interested in where we were from and what brought us to Chicago.

We took our turns in the chairs, getting our big-city haircuts, while they chattered good-naturedly about Chicago and business and asked about the drive. They really worked us over—electric clippers, razors, big powdered brushes and cold perfumed water. When I thought no one was looking, I reached back to rub my fingers upward against the bristle on the back of my neck.

Back in the lobby, Sweet looked at me and grinned. "If you tried to get on that gray lookin' and smellin' like you do, he'd buck you clear into the next province." Laughing, we all agreed he was right. I didn't look or smell like Henry McEwen, and he sure didn't look or smell like John Sweet.

Lew spoke up. "How would you like to get a look at some of the sights?" He'd been in Chicago on the rodeo circuit a few years back and knew what to see. We took our turns getting through the big revolving glass door and waved down a passing taxi. I was starting to get the hang of that door, but I still felt relief every time I survived it.

Lew gave the driver directions. Ten minutes later we were driving down State Street, the broadest street I had ever seen. On both sides the buildings were so tall that I felt like we were in a big, flat-bottomed, man-made canyon. The driver let us out in "the Loop," right in the middle of downtown. I could barely see the tops of the buildings. I craned my neck and started counting the stories on the tallest one when Lew said, "Just about sixty-five floors. Let's go in."

We entered the lobby and walked over to the elevators. Now *this* would be an elevator ride! On the top floor we went through a large glass door onto an observation platform.

I walked over to the chest-high concrete retaining wall and looked out and my mouth dropped open. I was enchanted. I couldn't believe Chicago's size! It spread farther than I could see to the west and south. To the north and east, clear to the horizon, was Lake Michigan. Icebreakers had cut a crisscross pattern through the ice. Ships of every description were moving among the broken pieces, coming and going with the coal, ore, grain, and other goods that were the lifeblood of this agricultural crossroads of the continent. Hundreds of other ships were tied at the docks. They all looked like miniatures from where we were. I remembered from my geography back in Raymond that the Canadian

Province of Ontario lay hundreds of miles north, touching this same lake where it turned east and joined Lake Huron. Even from sixty-five stories up, we could only see the first forty or fifty miles of it.

For more than half an hour we walked around all four sides of the observation platform. Lew pointed out the things of interest he knew about. We thought we could make out the stockyards to the south—now just a big, dark square on the earth. I looked down at the streets below, marveling at the tiny flecks that were people and the little moving oblong spots that were automobiles.

To the north I saw airplanes at what Lew called the airport. I made out long, straight strips—the runways where the planes took off and landed—and Lew told me the planes taking off now would be in New York before dark. I just shook my head at the wonder of it.

We rode the elevator back down to the street again. We visited the stock exchange, the World's Exposition Building, and the Wilson Building. I found out that in these huge buildings, most of the floors above the street level were filled with offices. How could there be a need for so many offices?

Lew asked if there was anything else in particular we would like to see, and I mentioned I wanted to buy something for my family. A short walk took us to a department store even bigger than the Emporium, although I didn't think that was possible. It was six stories tall, and each floor was devoted to a different kind of merchandise. We started at the top and worked our way down, doing a little preliminary shopping, seeing things we hadn't known existed, let alone how to use half of it. I didn't know yet what I'd buy, but whatever it was going to be, there was sure to be one of it in that department store.

Back out on the street we decided to go see a moving picture show. I had once seen one about twenty minutes long in Calgary and had enjoyed it. Half a block down the street we paid twenty-five cents each at the Roxy Theatre to see a fifty-minute silent movie about cowboys in Arizona.

The piano player who accompanied the moving pictures let us know when the villains were about to show up; he played louder and in a weird-sounding minor key. The story was about a train robber in the wild west. We had to smile when the sheriff and the posse went after the outlaw and his gang. We figured they ran their horses about halfway across the state of Arizona without a rest. They were firing six-shooters which, by our count, they could shoot at least twenty times without reloading. And that wasn't half of it. In the final chase, the outlaw turned in the saddle on his running horse and fired one shot at the posse, which was half a mile behind him. When two members of the posse fell off their horses, all four of us laughed right out loud. Where did the outlaw get that pistol? Twenty shots without reloading? Two guys half a mile back with one shot? What a pistol!

The sheriff finally shot the outlaw, which brought us to the dumbest scene in the entire movie. The bum died in the arms of the local schoolteacher, who for some reason liked him despite the fact that he was a robber and had shot half the posse. Now, how did she show up in the middle of the Arizona badlands, after a nonstop two-hundred-mile horse chase, looking like she was dressed for a church social?

Back out on the street, it took a while to get adjusted to the bright sunlight. We got our bearings and found a little hole-in-the-wall shop down the street where the owner sat behind a counter selling hot dogs and soft drinks. He smiled as he saw us coming and gave us his pitch—"A loaf of bread, a pound of meat, and all the mustard you can eat." We had a couple of hot dogs each and drank grape soda pop. It was fun, standing there on the street and eating, watching the people and the traffic go by. The owner was a real talker, but pretty nice. He kept a running conversation with us while we ate and waved to us when we left.

It was getting on into the afternoon, and Lew suggested we ride the subway back to our hotel. We walked down the stairs at a nearby station. Beneath the streets, with no natural light, electric bulbs glowed everywhere. Lew studied the schedules on the wall. He figured that with one transfer we could come within a block or two of the Drexel Arms.

We bought our tokens, dropped them in the turnstile, and walked onto the platform where we were to wait. Running into blackness to my left was the tunnel the train was to come from, and to my right, the same blackness closed down on where it would go. We heard the rumble start a couple of minutes before the coaches arrived. Then, with a great rush of air and sound, the train pulled in and stopped. The doors opened automatically and people poured out, then poured in, us among them.

As we careened through the tunnel, the lights from inside the car revealed that the tunnel walls were just two or three feet away. I got an idea of how a snake in a gopher burrow must feel. I'm sure the subway served a purpose, but just the same I couldn't help thinking that an accident could hurt a lot of people.

About four stops later Lew hustled us off. Quickly we climbed the stairs to street level, hurried about a block, and went back down into the subway to catch the second train. Two stops later we got off again and climbed back to street level. After looking around for several minutes, Lew admitted he was lost.

A policeman walking his beat straightened us out. He sent us to a platform twenty feet above the street, where we waited for one of those overhead trains. This time we did it right; the train took us to within two blocks of the hotel. We couldn't resist ribbing Lew about finding his way across a continent and then getting lost in Chicago.

It was getting close to four o'clock. Lew, Charlie, and Sweet decided to wait at the hotel until time for supper with Billy Daniels. I decided to visit a little shop I had noticed this side of the Emporium to get my hat cleaned and blocked.

The shop owner was an Italian. He smiled and invited me to watch him work. After removing the hand-braided leather hatband, he put the hat on a turntable and started it spinning. Using a foot pedal, he gave it regular blasts of steam, working the felt with a big brush and his free hand. Before long my hat was steamed and brushed clean. He put some sizing back into the felt and shaped the crown, and it looked like it had looked the day I bought it. After he finished he blew air on it for a minute and replaced the hatband. It cost two dollars, but that seemed like a bargain considering it was as good as new.

It was just after five when I got back to my room. I re-blocked my hat with the crease in front and put in on the closet shelf. My old clothes, including my heavy brown coat, were laid out on my bed, all cleaned and folded. My boots were beside the bed, shined so bright I hardly recognized them. Just as I finished putting everything on the shelf by the hat, the other three rapped on my door. It was time to head downstairs to meet Daniels.

The uniformed waiter took our supper orders while Daniels and Charlie started talking about the cattle business in southern Alberta. Daniels wanted to know everything—how many ranches, how big, how many cattle up on the range. Charlie did most of the answering, although the rest of us helped once in a while.

Daniels wrote down much of the information about owners and how he could reach them. He sure wasn't trying to keep his ideas a secret. He wanted to find someplace where he could get cheap range cattle during the off season. As a rule, range stock only hit the market in two big waves—spring roundup and fall roundup. But the fact is, there's a good market for them at the big sausage kitchens the entire year round. Daniels' idea was to get a couple more heavy shipments in the middle of the winter and summer. We didn't know how that idea would work out, but we could see the good sense of it. He asked us to think about it, to talk with the ranchers up home and get their reactions.

Later during our meal, Daniels asked about the cattle drive, and one of the first things he wanted to know about was the stampede.

"Ask Henry," Charlie said. "He's the one who reached the leaders first." Daniels turned to me and laid his fork down. Listening meant more than eating to this man.

I started with the nervous feeling we all had because of the wolf scare, and said how tense I felt going on duty in the dark at four o'clock that morning. I got to where the dawn was starting to show to the east and then the sudden whooshing sound Clark Lund and I heard as the first of the cattle broke bedground and started running. Then a rumbling sound, like thunder, as the entire herd hit full running stride. Our horses jumping and prancing; Clark and I grabbing the saddlehorns and swinging up while they were on the dead run; me giving the gray his head to work toward the edge of the herd; looking back for Clark but not seeing him; finally breaking free, kicking the gray to the hardest run we had ever made; reaching the leaders just as they began to slow. Then spinning the gray back into the herd, my heart almost stopped, afraid Clark was down; finally seeing him coming on Maude; yelling where was Fritz—and feeling my heart sink when Clark didn't know. Raising the gray into another full-stride run to the back of the herd; cutting west and finding the buckskin all but dead on her feet. Then finding Fritz Hoffman just after Sweet put the buckskin out of her pain.

I knew Daniels hadn't moved a muscle during the telling, but only when I finished did I notice what was going on around us. For fifteen or twenty feet around our table people had stopped eating and were sitting motionless, their food forgotten, silently hanging on every word.

When I realized they'd been listening to me I was embarrassed. I quickly brought my eyes back to my plate and bowed my head slightly. I didn't know what to do with all those eyes on me. I started to pick up my fork and then stopped, turning red. Charlie started to chuckle and Daniels glanced around, smiling. I think part of the spell of the story was because I was smooth-cheeked and young. Maybe the people couldn't believe a kid like me had come through such adventures.

"What was that about a wolf scare, Henry?" Daniels asked. All I wanted was to end the storytelling and find a way out, but that wasn't to be. I guess Sweet knew I was tongue-tied, because he chimed in.

"We never were sure if it was the same one, but we'd seen a big old gray wolf off and on, sniffin' at the herd for about three days, and . . ." He told the whole story, ending with ". . . and Henry here shot that old Lobo at sunset with his daddy's .45-70 Springfield at a range of 582 yards."

By now no one around us was even pretending to eat. A few had turned their chairs toward us. Even the waiter was standing to one side listening.

Lew told the next story, the one about going through the ice at the water tank. "The craziest story of the entire drive was me taking a bath. Charlie sent me and Henry out to break the ice on a big watering pond so the herd could get to the water, and . . ." He told the story in such a funny way that by the time he finished, all of us in that part of the restaurant were laughing. I didn't know Lew had such a humorous streak in him. But despite the way he told it, I think everyone knew how close we had come to losing both him and the brown horse.

We continued answering Daniels' questions right up through our pie. Charlie told the last one—the blizzard, and how Sweet found the only place for miles around where we could hold the cattle from drifting that night. And then finally, the people around us went back to their meals, buzzing and talking. Two men off to our left—one big, the other smaller—seemed to be enjoying it most of all. I wondered who they were.

It was clear Daniels had enjoyed the stories clear to his bones and would save them to be recalled over and over again. I felt a little sorry for him, knowing he had once been on drives like that himself. Now that was behind him forever.

Just before we broke up for the evening, Daniels turned to Charlie and his eyes got serious. "Would you consider doing me a personal favor? When you get back up there, would you find out if there might be a job open for a woman? A girl? Schoolteaching, or maybe bookkeeping?"

I had a pretty good idea where this was going.

"We can do that," Charlie replied. "What ye got in mind?"

"Phyllis."

"Phyllis? Ye have it in yer mind to send yer *daughter* up into that country?" That one even stopped Charlie.

"You saw her yesterday. You know the problem. Can you think of a better way to straighten her out? Will you ask around and write me?"

"Sure we will. No promises, but we'll try." He took the business card with the address that Daniels handed him, and put it inside his logbook.

A few minutes later, as we were breaking up, we agreed to meet Daniels in the lobby at three the next afternoon to get out money and sign a receipt for the cattle. There was a ripple of comment from the people around us. Some even thanked us and said goodbye. At the elevators, we thanked Daniels for the evening. He wouldn't listen to our thanks, saying he was the one who should thank us for the most enjoyable evening he'd had in ten years.

I sat awake in my room later that night, thinking about the evening. All those people in an expensive, classy restaurant, stopping to listen to stories about a cattle drive told by a fifteen-year-old kid and his companions. Daniels asking us to help him save his daughter by getting her away from a city where she had every opportunity in the world, so far as I could see. Get her into the prairie country to straighten her out.

Straighten her out? Up in Raymond? Was everyone going crazy? Or was I really the king of Fool's Hill, whatever that was?

By the time I drifted into a fitful sleep that night, I was the most confused, mixed-up kid in Chicago.

Chapter Eighteen

After breakfast, we gathered in Charlie's room to make a plan.

Daniels was to deliver a bank cashier's check in the amount of $50,762.50, plus $500 in cash. The total was $51,262.50. Charlie had quietly asked around and determined that the hotel safe was usually pretty good. But because a few things had turned up missing now and again, we couldn't take a chance on it. There was no point in putting the money in a bank, because we couldn't get it back out at four in the morning, which was when our train was leaving for Cut Bank. To wire that much money across an international border was expensive and would take too much time getting certifications, exchange rates, and clearances to disburse it at the far end. Even if we wanted to, there wasn't a bank in or even near Raymond that was hooked up with the international circuit of banks.

We were going to have to take the money home with us. Charlie figured the best way was to put it in a money belt. He was sure nothing was going to happen, but our job wouldn't be finished until we got the money in the bank in Raymond. We weren't about to take any unnecessary chances between here and there.

Charlie and Lew went out to buy a money belt and look for the Western Union Telegraph Station. As soon as we had the money, they wanted to tell Mr. Baker the amount and when we expected to be back in Raymond. Meanwhile Sweet and I decided to go shopping. I still wanted to buy some things for my family.

I figured the Emporium had one of everything in the world, so we walked the four blocks and pushed our way through the big glass doors. I guess we spent an hour and a half in there, just looking at things. I had to wrestle a little with myself about getting anything for Jacob. Down deep I wanted to, but I could still feel the sting of him lecturing me all the time. I had to argue with myself a little over the question.

I finally bought him a pocket knife—a small pearl-handled one with two blades, made in Solingen, Germany, of good carbon steel. I thought he might enjoy a gentleman's knife to clean and square his nails, instead of the big clasp knife he had used since I could remember.

I bought Elmer a stainless steel bit for his favorite bridle. The bit was slightly curved to give some control without hurting the horse's mouth. He had wanted one like that for a long time. It was of high quality, made by the Hereford Company out of Texas.

I had to look quite a while before I found what I wanted for mother. It was a beautiful comb, hand carved from a seashell. I thought she might like to have something, just one thing, that was nice and ladylike and hers alone.

The last thing I bought was the most expensive. I spent a whole week's wages to buy the family a banjo. I couldn't count how many times both mother and Jacob had commented on how much it would mean to have a banjo in the family—something we could all learn so we could make our own music at home. They liked the twangy sound and rhythms, and it seemed to them like no band was complete without a banjo. I bought a good one with a solid, hard-shell case that locked.

I paid for the gifts. The clerk wrapped each one separately and packed the three small ones in a cardboard box.

Charlie and Lew had found the telegraph station and were waiting at the hotel when Sweet and I returned with our purchases. In the restaurant as we ate our midday meal, Charlie told us about the plan for the trip home. Our train would leave at 4:10 the next morning from Grand Central Station. It was a passenger train going only as far as Cut Bank, Montana. From Cut Bank we would ride the caboose on a cattle train headed to Sweetgrass, arriving there early enough to make nearly twenty miles on horseback before dark. We would be home the next afternoon—four days from now.

At that moment Raymond seemed a long way from Chicago and the luxury we had been enjoying.

At three o'clock we met Billy Daniels in the lobby. A few people there who remembered the stories from the previous night said hello to us. The two men who had seemed to enjoy them most, the big one and the smaller one, spoke to me and I returned their greeting. Remembering how they enjoyed the stories, laughing about Lew getting his icy bath, I wondered if they had worked cattle sometime in their lives.

Up in Daniels' office, our business didn't take long. Daniels handed Charlie a cashier's check for $50,762.50 and Charlie examined it, satisfied it was genuine. Daniels counted out five hundred dollars in twenty-dollar bills, bringing the total to $51,262.50. It was all there. Charlie signed a receipt for the money and a bill of sale for the cattle. The two men shook hands and the transaction was complete. There was a minute or two of the usual good-natured small talk, and then Charlie stood.

"I have to get to Western Union and send a telegram to Mr. Baker. It's been a pleasure doin' business with ye, Billy. I'll remember yer interest in the cow business up in my part of the country. I'll write ye about it one way or the other when I find out the thinkin' of the ranchers up there. I'll also write ye about yer daughter Phyllis."

"I'll expect any of you to come see me if you ever get to Chicago again," Daniels responded. "I've enjoyed dealing with you. Forget the hotel bill—that's on me, as I said. What you've done for me personally has paid the bill ten times over."

The four of us headed back down the hall to Charlie's room. Once inside, he spoke in low tones. "I'm thinkin' there probably won't be much to worry about. But if anyone *does* have ideas about gettin' their hands on this money, they'll probably expect it to be in the hotel safe or hidden in one of our rooms. They'll probably think about my room first and Lew's second." He drew a small, long package out of his inside coat pocket. "So I think we should put the money in the money belt and the money belt on Henry."

139

"You're right, Charlie," Lew said. "Henry would be the last one anyone would suspect." Sweet added his agreement.

I was getting the same feeling I had when they decided I was going to whup Toothy Jack and the Swede in checkers back in Sweetgrass. Don't I get a vote on *any* of this?

Charlie held half the cash money out for travel expenses and carefully slipped everything else into the belt. I pulled out my shirttail and unbuttoned the front of my long-handles, and Charlie slipped the money belt around my middle and buckled it closed. With my shirttail tucked in, you couldn't tell it was on me.

But *I* knew it was on me. I felt like a walking target—like I was wearing a big sign that said HENRY'S GOT THE MONEY IN A MONEY BELT.

Charlie and Lew assured me it would be fine. Then they headed for the telegraph office to send the telegram to Mr. Baker.

I looked at Sweet, trying out a casual expression for my face, like everything was normal. He busted out laughing.

"Henry," he said, "you look like the cat that ate the canary. You got to forget that thing is there and look normal. You need practice." He put his arm around my shoulder. "Come on, let's go find a couple of boxes—we need to pack up before morning."

I tried a different casual expression as we went to the front desk. Sweet asked where we could find a couple of cardboard boxes big enough for our trail clothes and enough cord to tie them shut. The desk clerk pointed toward a storage room and said, "Ask the man in there." Then he looked at me sort of funny and said "Are you all right?"

"Who, me? Uh, yeah, yessir, I'm all right. I'm fine, just fine." I sounded so dumb! I just knew the clerk was thinking, "That kid has fifty-one thousand bucks tied around his middle." I was fast learning that looking casual was the hardest work I'd ever done. Sounding casual was even worse.

We packed most everything up, the presents I had bought, too, and then went down for supper in the hotel restaurant. We took a little more time than usual. I memorized everything around me, knowing mother would want to hear all she could about staying in a luxury hotel in Chicago.

Part way through the meal, an odd little thing happened. Sweet paused with his fork halfway to his mouth. I glanced up to see what caught his eye. He was looking at those two men, the big one and the smaller one, who were sitting nearby and talking to each other kind of low. Something had hit Sweet wrong, but I didn't know what, so I just went on eating, and a few minutes later they left. When we finished our pie, we rose to leave with nothing particular in mind, just enjoying being filled with good food.

Charlie and Lew were already in the room where music was performed. Sweet walked over to look in the door and see what the entertainment was, and just at that moment the two men approached me and stopped to make conversation. I guess they'd been in the lobby letting their suppers settle.

"We sure enjoyed those stories last night. Sounded like you men came through some pretty exciting times, getting that herd of cattle here." It was the big man, smiling. He seemed real friendly and I smiled back.

"We didn't exactly think of them as exciting when some of them happened. More like scary."

"Mr. Daniels paid a pretty good price for them, we hear."

"Yeah, a fair price. Paid off today, matter of fact."

"Well, it's sure been nice hearing about the adventure. Good luck on your way back home."

They left just as Sweet moseyed back over toward me. He'd decided not to join Charlie and Lew for the music, and he knew I didn't go for it much either, so he'd signaled to Charlie that we were going upstairs to turn in.

He was working a toothpick in his mouth as we crossed the foyer when he made a casual statement that made me feel like my blood had turned to ice.

"With nobody knowin' we got paid off today, we don't have to worry about that money. Just leave the belt around your middle tonight, and . . ."

I stopped dead in my tracks.

"Someone does know, Sweet. I think I told 'em just now."

I could feel a controlled tension in him instantly. He took the toothpick out of his mouth and spoke quietly.

"Who? Let me guess. The big guy and the little guy."

I couldn't speak. I just nodded yes.

"I had a hunch at supper they were takin' an unhealthy interest, talkin' low and pointin' at us."

141

That explained the funny look that had crossed his face during supper.

"You got the belt?" he asked.

"Right here."

"Good, because my guess is they're up in our rooms right now lookin' for it. If that's true, now's the time to catch 'em red-handed. Let's go." He started toward the staircase, moving pretty fast, with me right behind him. On the way up the stairs he told me to see if my room had been searched while he did the same with his.

I tried my door. Still locked. I used my key, walked in, and flipped on the lights, letting the door close behind me. Nothing appeared to be out of place. I checked the bathroom and closet and then heard the sound of a key in my door lock. In the next twenty seconds things happened so fast I didn't have time to get scared.

I turned the lights out and moved close to the door, determined that whoever came through would take at least one good shot from out of the dark. Then I heard rapid footsteps in the hallway. The key stopped turning; I heard muffled words, then the sound of someone getting hit real hard. A body slammed into my door and started to slide down it. Something inside me snapped. I had to know what was going on! I twisted the lever on my side of the lock and jerked the door open, ready for whatever was happening.

It was the smaller man who had been knocked into my door, and he was now trying without any success to get his feet back under him and stand up. To my right in the hallway I saw Sweet's back and, over his shoulder, the big man from the lobby. He had at least six inches and fifty pounds on Sweet, and I wasted a split second fearing for Sweet. The big guy got in one clumsy swing, but Sweet slid under it, sinking his left hand about a foot into that big paunch and pausing just long enough to be sure his right hand was accurate. Sweet's fist only traveled about eighteen inches before it hit him with every pound he had. Sweet grunted when he connected, right on the point of the chin. The big man went down like a sack of wheat. Sweet stood there a moment in case he got back up, but it didn't look to me like he'd be going anywhere for quite a while.

About then, the little man Sweet had downed first was up on one knee, making ready to go after Sweet from behind. He didn't know I was there. I grabbed his hair and jerked him over backward, banging his head on the floor as hard as I could. The way he lay there, for a second I was afraid I'd killed him.

Sweet turned around at the noise. He hadn't been aware that I'd gotten into the fight. He knew he hadn't hit the little man hard enough to keep him down, and he looked ready for another round. For just a moment I saw the thunder and lightning in his eyes that I'd always known was inside him. Then it faded.

He spoke to me quietly, breathing heavy. "You all right, Henry? Still got the money belt?"

"Yeah, I'm fine. The money's right here." I patted my shirt front. My blood was still up from the brief fight. Sweet looked at the little man and then at me. "What did you hit him with?"

"The floor. I banged his head on the floor."

Sweet stepped over him, looking at the key still in the door lock. He drew it out, examined it closely, and read the words stamped on it aloud. "Master Key. DAH." He thought for a second. "DAH is Drexel Arms Hotel."

He started down the hall, calling back over his shoulder. "You watch these two. If they try to get up, hit 'em with the floor. I'll be back in about three minutes."

While he was gone a man and woman started out of their room, took one look at the bodies in the hall, turned white, and disappeared right back inside. They must have thought I'd just killed them.

Four or five minutes later Sweet reappeared, literally dragging that uppity desk clerk, and followed by Charlie, Lew, and another man I didn't recognize. A few shocked, frightened people were peeking around the corner of the stairwell to watch the proceedings.

Sweet's manner with the clerk was anything but gentle. "You got about three minutes before one of them comes around. When they do, the first question I put to 'em is how they got that master key. The second question is who told 'em where our rooms were. If you make one peep before I get the answers, you're the next guy that gets laid out on the floor. You understand that?"

The clerk was already white as a sheet. The front of his shirt and vest were messed up. I could only guess what had happened.

Sweet hunkered down by the little man, talking and lightly

slapping him to wake him up. When he came to he groaned, gingerly touching the back of his head to feel the knot the floor and I had put there.

The clerk looked petrified for a moment; then his sheer terror forced the words out. "These hooligans are going to lie. They're going to say I gave them the key. It isn't true. I didn't do it! They stole it!"

Sweet rose and took a step toward the clerk. I saw the lightning in his eyes again.

"If that's true, why didn't you go to your safe and look for the master key when I asked for it just now? You want to know why? You knew it was gone. You'd given it to them! You figured they could fleece fifty thousand dollars from us four country boys and cut you in for some of it, with nobody the wiser. What was your cut going to be?"

The clerk's teeth were chattering. "Nothing! I deny it all. If they had the key, they stole it."

Sweet thrust his face so close that the clerk couldn't miss the lightning in his eyes, and I know he heard the thunder starting. His fingers nervously reached up and touched the breast of his coat, then dropped again. Sweet caught the movement.

"You going to tell us they stole it while you were on duty? You want us to believe that two men could come behind the desk with you, work the combination on the safe, steal the master key, close the safe, and leave without you knowin' it?" Sweet glanced at us. "Any of you going to believe that?"

The house detective shook his head. The big man was still out cold, but the little one groaned and tried to sit up. Sweet grabbed him by the lapels and lifted him to his feet. "Mister, can you understand me?"

He looked at Sweet and cringed, remembering the last thing he had seen before he went down. "Yes. Yes, I understand."

"When did the clerk give you the master key for this robbery? What did he tell you about who was in which room?"

"He slipped it to us just after you all sat down for supper. He . . ."

The clerk started to wail. "He's a liar. I don't know anything about it. I . . ." He stopped. Again he reached up and touched his coat at his left breast, and this time Sweet jerked the clerk's coat open and yanked out the wallet inside. The frantic clerk lunged for Sweet and shouted, "That's mine—you got no right!"

Sweet didn't say a word. He held the clerk by his shirt front and tossed the wallet to the house detective. "I think we're on to somethin'. Have a look."

Inside the wallet was a letter addressed to Daniels' bank on stationery that said Baker Ranch, Alberta, Canada. It stated that the bearer, Charles MacDonald, was authorized to cash any checks made out to the Baker ranch, and it was signed by David Baker. The whole thing was a stupid, obvious forgery.

The house detective handcuffed the clerk, and the police arrived to take the three conspirators away. The buzzing and talk from the onlookers faded as we went into Charlie's room and shut the door.

"Are ye all right? The money belt?" I could see the deep concern in Charlie.

"I'm fine. The money belt is right here. They never got that far. Sweet stopped 'em."

"What tipped you off, Sweet?" Lew asked.

"Those two guys have been hangin' around an awful lot ever since we got here, payin' too much attention to us and our business. They left the restaurant before we did tonight, which was unusual for them. When I found out they'd talked to Henry and knew about the payoff today, I figured they were up here goin' through our rooms for the money. I think Henry and I came up while they were in either Charlie's or Lew's room. When I finished checking my room and started for Henry's, they were at his door tryin' to get in. We had a scuffle and Henry and me talked 'em out of it."

Lew's eyes sobered. "Could Daniels have been in on this? The clerk must have known quite a bit to have printed stationery and forged papers ready to go."

I couldn't believe my ears.

"I don't think so," Charlie answered. "He gave us a cashier's check, and the only proper endorsement on it was mine. No, I'm sure Daniels was straight. The clerk probably got most of his information just watchin' Daniels operate here fer the past couple of years, and lookin' at the hotel register where I signed in as a representative of the Baker ranch. Wouldn't take much imagination from there."

Sweet turned to Lew. "Might want to take a look around your room before you turn in," he suggested. "I think you'll see they were inside."

Charlie glanced around. "Yeah, I can see they were in mine. But there's nothin' of any value here except my trail clothes, and they're still on the shelf."

Charlie could see the question on my face. "Keep the money belt, Henry. We guessed pretty good so far. I'll not worry further about it. Are we ready to turn in? Three o'clock comes pretty early."

I had to say something to Charlie. "I feel pretty dumb, not knowin' to keep my mouth shut about the money, Mr. MacDonald. I won't do it again."

"Might have been a blessing, Henry. They were going to try fer that money sometime before we left. Maybe yer mistake ruined their plan by lettin' us pick the time and place fer the showdown."

There was one more piece of this whole thing I didn't get to see, and I wanted to know. "Mr. MacDonald, what happened downstairs? That clerk looked like he'd stared death in the face when Sweet brought him up here."

"He had. Sweet came into the parlor and told Lew and me to come with him and be witnesses, and from the look on his face we didn't ask no questions. We just followed him to the clerk's desk. Sweet asked to see the master key, which the clerk refused. Sweet grabbed him by his coat front and hauled him right over the top of the desk. He held him so his toes were barely touching the floor and asked him again. He refused again. There were about twenty people standin' around the lobby gettin' pretty nervous. Sweet told Lew to get the house detective and we all came upstairs, Sweet draggin' the clerk along by his collar. Ye know the rest."

I tried to picture it all in my mind. He'd jerked that uppity clerk over the desk like a sack of potatoes! Oh, how I wished I'd been there to see that!

We said good-night to each other and went to our rooms. Thinking over the startling events of the evening, I could hardly believe the way my visit to Chicago was coming to a close. I had been expecting excitement in the big city, but nothing quite like this. I shook my head, chuckled to myself, and headed for the bathroom. Excitement or no, nothing would stop me from taking one last shower.

Chapter Nineteen

I was sitting alone in the day coach, unaware of the faint clicking of the wheels and the constant, slight swaying of the train as we sped westward across North Dakota. I was staring out the window at the frozen, snow-covered hills and plains without really seeing them.

Boarding the train in the gigantic barn they called Grand Central Station in Chicago yesterday morning, I had expected to feel good. We had the money and we were on the way home, with two days to enjoy the adventure of riding a passenger train. But somehow something was missing.

The dining car was fine, with its good food and service. The smoking coach had magazines all laid out and a shelf of books to read. Going to bed in my upper berth last night had been a challenge. After the porters made up the bed, I climbed the little ladder and rolled in. I closed the curtain, but I could hear people—both men and women—walking up and down the aisle and talking late into the night. If they expected me to pull off my drawers with that going on, they were crazy. I took my shirt off but slept in my new trousers, long-handles, and socks.

I had been one of the first to get up this morning, and I washed up and combed my hair in the GENTLEMEN'S REST ROOM. Maybe that's what the sign said, but what went on inside had nothing to do with resting. Some of these signs were purely comical.

149

As the train carried me closer to home, my thoughts returned more and more to the dark, frosty morning more than three weeks ago when I'd left. My father was inside that home, and I left it feeling that I had to get away from him, I couldn't stand being there another season. Then why had I felt pain in my heart and mind when I got the chance to leave? And how did I feel now that I was going back? Despite my best effort to push it away, a haunting thought kept thrusting itself at me: there's something wrong, Henry, and it's important.

I had to get to the bottom of it, or go crazy.

So I came to the day coach alone, resolved in my heart to find peace of mind or die sitting there. I'd been there for an hour, pulling out every feeling and thought I had, trying to put them together so it all made sense. But it was coming all wrong. I was pretty sure that staying in Raymond was like accepting death before I was dead. Expecting Jacob to do anything but continue making my life pure misery was a waste of time. So it would seem like leaving Jacob and Raymond was the answer.

But Daniels had once felt that way. Now he had everything I thought I wanted. I *couldn't* bear the thought of spending the rest of my life around my father in Raymond. Yet Daniels was familiar with that kind of life, and he obviously thought it would be better for Phyllis than life in Chicago. If she stayed in the city she'd break his heart, sure as anything. Sometimes I got the feeling the city itself was breaking his heart, that he was sorry he'd come.

What was I missing?

I was jolted from my deep thoughts by a rough, gnarled, friendly old hand settling on my shoulder. I shook my head to clear it and looked up at Charlie's weathered, wrinkled face and blue-gray eyes.

He sat down opposite me, and for a time we silently watched the Black Hills of North Dakota steadily slip past to the rhythm of the clicking rails and the motion of the car.

"Suppose we'll be able to find work fer the Daniels girl?" He said it quietly, wistfully, almost like he was talking to himself.

Why did he choose her? Of all the things he could have talked about, why Phyllis? It seemed like he somehow knew I'd been thinking about that situation.

I spoke thoughtfully. "If you did find her a job, I don't think she'd come. And if she came, I don't think she'd last a week."

"Maybe so. But maybe that ain't the question. Maybe the question is helpin' her dad take one more try at wakin' her up."

Waking her up? From what? If she was any wider awake, somebody would give her a good licking just out of general principles.

Charlie shook his head slightly and a faraway look crept into his eyes. I had never seen this side of him. Instinct told me to be quiet and listen.

"Funny how things go. Eighteen years ago, Daniels thought he saw a chance to step up in the world by movin' from a ranch in Wyoming to Chicago. Figured he could provide his wife and daughter and son with the good things—a fine home, money, education in the city. He did it. Now he's not so sure how smart it was. His son is okay, but he'd give a lot to save his daughter from ruinin' herself."

He fell into silence. His eyes reflected memories and thoughts from times and places deep in the past, known only by him.

"Strange how it all works out. A man tries to take hold of life and do what he thinks he should. But somehow, one way or the other, life winds up testin' him. Sometimes it takes away his loved ones, and sometimes it takes away his health. Sometimes it takes away his wealth and sometimes it gives him too *much* wealth. I ain't figured out yet which is worse. I get the feelin' every once in a while that reachin' yer own dream isn't really what the Almighty is most interested in. I think maybe He sets a higher price on how ye stand up to it when life just keeps tryin' to put ye down."

He paused, glancing down at his hands—scarred, big knuckled, hard, strong, capable. He rubbed them together for a moment. "Wish I'd had a better hold on that thought thirty years ago."

I didn't move a muscle, hardly able to believe Charlie might be about to tell me his own story.

"Yer father Jacob and I and a few others thought the new, virgin land around Raymond was what we were lookin' fer. That was more than thirty years ago. I brought my Ruth and my two children, Rachel and James. Jacob brought yer mother, Eunice, and a couple of yer oldest brothers and sisters. We built homes fer our families and started in to make our dreams real, carvin' somethin' fine out of a wilderness. This was before the government built the big irrigation canal. It was long before Jesse Knight and his sons built the sugar factory outside of town that went broke and closed down."

His eyes dropped and his voice went husky. "It was 1894 when the smallpox hit us. The epidemic started in the Blood Indians and then swept through most of the southern Province. We didn't know how to fight it. The Mounties came to help, and we all did what we could. It killed nearly half the Indians and a lot of the settlers. It took my Ruth and Rachel and James. Yer father and mother helped me bury them."

His eyes stayed down. I hardly breathed. I had a lump in my throat seeing on his face the worst pain he had ever endured. He rubbed the sleeve of his coat across his eyes before going on.

"I couldn't stand up to it. I didn't know how to handle it. I didn't have it in me to start over. I lost about two years drinkin', wastin' my life, before I finally woke up and realized what I was doin' to myself. I never found the courage to remarry and start a family again, but I slowly steadied myself up and started bein' responsible."

I could see that his eyes were red. He fixed his gaze on the rim of a distant hill. "With yer father, the test came different. Four times I know of, life has taken everything from him except his wife and his children. I know about the time he didn't understand the need for filing the land purchase papers in the Provincial Recorder's Office, and it cost him his land. I know about the three times he lost every animal he had in severe winters. He started over again all three times. The last one was about ten years ago, when ye would have been about five, Henry. That winter the cold killed almost everything on the prairie. Coyotes and wolves was comin' right into the ranch yards to kill and eat dogs, cats, anything they could get. One mornin' yer father heard wolves snufflin' at the kitchen door in the dark. He killed five of them with the Winchester. The last one was too far out in the dark. I was in town when yer father sold the hides, fer five dollars each. It was the first cash money he'd seen in a long time. Can ye remember that, Henry?"

I swallowed, nodding yes. I would never forget waking up to the crashing bang of five rapid shots, later going outside to see the five dead wolves strung out from the kitchen door almost to the shed. But no one had ever told me we lost all our livestock that winter, or that the pelt money was the first cash father had seen in weeks.

"I know how it hurt him, watchin' the years come and go and never being able to give yer mother the nice things he wanted to give her. He knew what it was doin' to her, how she went sort of dead inside when she lost the baby Darwin. Jacob told me many times that he felt like a failure, that he couldn't provide fer his own. I remember three or four years ago him comin' to town with just nine dollars to buy somethin' fer you kids fer Christmas. Nine dollars. Twenty-five years of work, and all he had was nine dollars fer Christmas. He could hardly stand the pain. I know he drank more than he should have that day, and I know he was ashamed of it. But how does a man come home and tell all this to his kids and their mother? Yer father wept that night. It was me who helped him home, Henry."

I was shocked past any words. I sat there staring, struck dumb that he knew about that Christmas, that he understood and loved Jacob, and didn't condemn or judge him.

"But unlike me, yer father never buckled. He never quit. He took his losses, and he accepted his own weaknesses, and he stayed and struggled."

At last Charlie brought his gaze down from the distant rim. He looked at me, then back out the window. "The world has changed around him and me. Our time is pretty well past. We don't know how to deal with this new world of telegraphs and telephones and big cities and automobiles. The lessons we learned, the things we know—they belong to a time that's just slipping into memories. We both know it, and that's what weighs so heavy on yer father now. He sees himself all over again in ye—probably more than in any of yer brothers. He knows yer bright and ambitious, that ye want to be off testin' yer own wings. And he knows that's the way it should be. He just doesn't want ye to get stuck on Fool's Hill and ruin yerself."

There it was! Fool's Hill! I couldn't say a word, couldn't think. My mind was swamped, stunned with what he was telling me. How could I have lived right there with my own father and never seen the man Charlie had just laid out for me? It felt for a second or two like my mind would come to pieces. And then Charlie had hit me right between the eyes with the same expression Jacob had used, "Fool's Hill." What did he and my father know that made them talk about Fool's Hill?

"Henry, yer father wants ye to find yer own way, yer own life. He knows it probably won't be in Raymond, but that's not important. What *is* important is that ye understand somethin'. No matter where ye decide to go, Jacob has tried to teach ye the things that are important—like bein' responsible, and havin' enough love and respect fer yer wife and family that ye won't cave in when yer test comes. More than anything he just wishes he could talk to ye—tell ye the things he's learned that he thinks are important."

For the first time Charlie looked at me as if he expected me to say something, but I couldn't speak. Every thought I'd ever had, everything I'd sorted out in my mind as being firm and fixed, was up in the air and then coming back down in different places. I felt like all the old things were somehow new, that I'd never seen them before.

"Yer father is a man worth listenin' to, Henry. I know. During those two wasted years after Ruth and the children were gone, Jacob took the time now and again to find me and talk to me. Just talk to me."

I saw the slightest wrinkle come into his forehead, like he was trying to judge whether he'd said what he wanted to say. He started to get up, but I couldn't let him go just yet. I *had* to know more. Impulsively I grasped his arm and blurted it out. "Charlie, goin' back to the day we finished the roundup and you and the men were standin' not far from the fire, decidin' what to do. My father was there. Do you remember?"

"I do." He settled back into his seat.

"What was my father sayin', Charlie? What was he sayin' about me?"

Charlie pursed his lips for a minute, carefully calling back the memory, looking for words that would say it as honestly as it could be said.

"He was sayin' ye needed to be away so ye could see yer home real clear and plain. And he told me ye had the makins of a top drover."

I sat there stunned, unable to speak or move.

"He asked me to take ye on the drive, knowin' I had never taken a boy just turned fifteen on such an assignment. I told him with that many cattle and nine men to be responsible fer, I didn't think I could risk it. He said ye'd pull yer own weight, that I could depend on ye. It was me that had fears about ye, not yer father. I took ye because I know Jacob McEwen. If he said I could depend on ye, then I could. And he was right. Ye've done a man's job, Henry, and ye've done it well. Maybe I've been given a way to repay him a little fer what he did fer me years ago. I hope so."

I sat quiet and motionless, wondering how I could live fifteen years and still be so bone dumb.

Charlie continued. "Now, maybe I can find a way to help Billy Daniels with Phyllis. Everyone has to cross over the top of Fool's Hill sometime in their life."

"Charlie, what's Fool's Hill? What did Jacob mean and what do you mean by Fool's Hill?"

He looked at me and saw me begging for the piece that was missing—the one I had to have. I wasn't going to be worth anything to anybody until I understood.

"Fool's Hill is the hill that every one of us has to cross to get from the child's side of life to the grown-up side. Seein' things the way they are instead of from the selfish kid's side. That includes seein' ourselves, with all of our strengths and weaknesses, so we can have some compassion and understanding and forgiveness fer the faults of everyone else. Some make it over Fool's Hill and some don't. Right now, Phyllis Daniels is stuck on the very top. Ye can tell by the way she thinks she's lookin' down both sides of it on just about everybody else in the world—thinkin' she knows more than any one of us or all of us put together. Particularly her dad. And that's as big a fool as you'll find in this world, Henry. It's a tough journey over that hill, but we all have to make it, regardless of the age or time or place we're born, big city or small country town. I feel sorry fer Phyllis. If I can help Daniels, I will."

It all washed over me so fast and so deep it took my breath away. There it was! The hill we all had to climb so we could get from the cocky, know-it-all kid's side to the grown-up side of life. Getting over that hill is the important thing, not staying stuck on top. After all the troubled feelings and confusion, things seemed so clear now I couldn't believe I'd been right in the middle of it without seeing it. If Fool's Hill ever had a king, I knew I'd worn the crown for a long, long time.

He leaned forward and laid his hand on my knee, looking into my eyes for just a moment. I know he saw the beginnings of the understanding he'd tried so hard to give me. I watched his eyes change, a hint of smile beginning to show. In his face I saw approval. But most of all I saw a look of deep satisfaction, and it made me want to bow my head and cry. I knew Charlie had just done for me what he'd been denied doing for his own James and Rachel when the Almighty took them. Deep in his heart he'd yearned for those two youngsters, felt a need to love and help them that he'd thought he would never get the chance to express. He needed to help me as much as I needed his help. Suddenly I remembered what he'd said just a few minutes earlier. "Strange how it all works out . . ."

I knew the magic of the time we had shared was past. It belonged just to me and Charlie, and I'd never have another like it in my life. I looked the old Scot in the eyes for just a few moments more, knowing he understood what a priceless thing he'd done for me and how I loved him for it. That was enough for both of us. Words would only have gotten in the way.

"It's gettin' pretty deep in the day. Guess I'll go find Sweet and Lew and be back in a while to get ye fer supper." He said it almost like he didn't want to leave.

He walked back down the aisle toward the car where the others were. Watching him as he disappeared, I felt absolutely certain of one thing. The new world Charlie had given me had almost nothing to do with the old one I'd been living in when he had walked into the railroad car twenty minutes earlier.

Chapter Twenty

Moving north and a little west, the four of us reined our horses down from an easy lope to a walk. We were silent, each riding with his own thoughts. We were nearly to the fork where Sweet and Lew and Charlie would continue north toward Raymond while I angled a little more west toward my home, now less than an hour away.

For two days, ever since my talk with Charlie, I had been quiet, working my way into the new world that had opened up in my mind. Lew and Sweet knew something had happened. They respected my need for the privacy of my own thoughts. I'd done my share of the few things that needed done in Sweetgrass, but I had to force myself to it, and I hadn't had much to say.

I'll never forget how good it felt, way down deep, to see the big gray horse again. Abraham had taken good care of him. We changed out of the city clothes into our clean trail clothes in Abraham's little shack, surprised when we put on our big hats. The hotel barber had taken too much hair, causing the hats to sit way low on our heads. We all had the same problem—our heads looked too small.

We thanked Abraham after we'd saddled up and tied the little sack of grub on Charlie's saddle. Back in my boots and spurs, with my chaps on, wearing the heavy brown coat, the scarf wrapped high, and the gray under me again—there aren't words to tell of the feeling.

Since we left Sweetgrass I'd been going through a process in my mind that was now coming so fast I couldn't catch up with it. I'd think of mother or father, or Elmer, or Raymond, and it was like I was seeing them for the first time. About an hour later I'd think of them again—and it was new once more; I'd see strengths and weaknesses that I'd never noticed before. Then twenty minutes later it would start all over again. It had been going on like that for two days. I was starting to get the hang of it, but it was bringing me face to face with a startling and scary thought.

A month ago I had ridden this trail away from Raymond, convinced that Elmer and Jacob needed to do some changing, that life in Raymond was a waste of time. Now, riding the same trail back, I was beginning to realize that the changing that was needed was in *me*. There were some pretty special people in Raymond, some of them in my own family. And that little zero of a town had started to look pretty special itself. Why had I never seen the strength and faith and endurance of the people there? It startled me every time I thought of it. How could I have lived fifteen years so cocksure I had everything all figured out? How had I missed seeing what I was finally beginning to see? I wondered what else I'd missed, and how big a fool I'd make of myself before I got it all straight.

Tied up with all of this was a strange feeling. Like magic, I was seeing a new Henry. And try as I would, I could hardly remember the old one. I was seeing qualities in myself both good and bad, strong and weak. I decided I could probably change some things, but others I wasn't so sure about.

That's what was scaring me. I'd never doubted before that I could do anything I set my mind to. But maybe there *was* something I couldn't do, at least not without a struggle—change myself! I thought about my father and Elmer, the times I'd criticized them for their weaknesses, been hard on them because they couldn't seem to change. Oh, how I wished I'd never done that. How I wished! I felt an ache in my heart that was almost more than I could bear.

When I left on the cattle drive, I'd figured on riding back to Raymond like a conquering hero, to show my father he'd been wrong about me. I'd saved up all those stories just to impress father and Elmer: Henry's a hero, grown up and capable of doing a man's job, pretty smart and important. I had figured to dump that all over them.

Instead I was riding back humbled, stripped of pride. I felt ashamed I'd ever thought of telling them those stories to prove they were wrong and I was right. Now I didn't want to tell them *any* stories. I only wanted to say I'd been a young, blind fool who needed their forgiveness and help.

Suddenly I became aware that Charlie had pulled his horse down just a little. We were riding along four abreast, me on the left end next to Sweet. Two riders were angling in from Charlie's side to meet us. At first I thought they were local range hands out to welcome us back. But as they approached, we saw they were strangers. One was blocky and one was thin. They wore old clothes and looked like they hadn't shaved in quite a while. Something was spooky about this whole setup, and I sensed that Lew and Sweet felt it too. Sweet had that narrow-eyed look I'd seen as he tore into that big robber back in the hotel in Chicago.

They raised their right hands in greeting as they came quartering in.

"Howdy, gents. I'm Charlie MacDonald. Don't believe I know ye." Charlie was looking holes through these two. He knew something was wrong.

The blocky one pulled his horse to a stop just in front of Charlie and pointed straight west. "We're just out ridin' scout for that herd comin' right over there." Without thinking all four of us turned our heads west. There was no herd. When we turned back to face them my heart all but stopped.

The man who had spoken was holding a .44 Colt, and the other one was cocking a sawed-off double-barreled shotgun.

Less than five miles from Raymond, and we were going to lose it all!

I was looking at those two renegades, but what I saw was the eyes and faces of fifty ranchers who had each put twenty or thirty years of their life's work into our hands. I could remember their faces when we broke the herd from bedground the morning we left. Their expressions had been almost like a prayer: "Please get these critters delivered and bring the money back. We got wives and kids and hopes and dreams ridin' on you men."

Grinning insolently, the blocky man spoke like he was talking

159

to dumb animals. "Now just rest easy and nobody gets hurt. If anyone makes a move we don't understand, Mr. MacDonald here gets shot, no questions asked. Get the picture?"

Both guns swiveled to point at Charlie.

"All right. That's just fine." He was still grinning like he enjoyed playing with us. "I expect Mr. MacDonald has the money, so I'll ask him once, very kindly, to just drop it on the ground, and then you gentlemen can go on into Raymond. Mr. MacDonald, move very slowly so we don't misunderstand what you're doing with your hands. We see anything that even resembles a weapon, you're a dead side of beef. Go ahead "

Charlie didn't have the money. I did. It was still in the money belt around my middle. Charlie didn't move or say a word. I believe he'd have traded his life to save the ranchers who had trusted us.

The thief quit smiling and his face got real ugly. He barked his next words. "I count to ten and we shoot MacDonald. Then right down the row until we find out who's got that money. One. Two. Three . . ."

I didn't doubt they'd shoot Charlie. Wild thoughts raced through my head, a hundred every second. Then an image stayed with me. I saw my father's face in the yellow glow of the kerosene lamp out in the shed the night I was packing, and I heard his last advice before I left. "Remember who you are. Do your job."

And right there, facing the worst odds I'd ever seen, one of those rare feelings washed over me, the kind so powerful a guy knows he'll never be the same again. It went clear to the marrow in my bones. It was pride. Pride in my father, my family, the folks in Raymond—pride in who they were and what they stood for. I was the most surprised kid on the face of this earth. It's the last thing I expected to feel, sitting there on the gray looking down the barrel of a .44 and the muzzle of a shotgun.

I'm Jacob McEwen's kid! I'm going to do my job! And these saddle bums aren't going to steal my people's hopes and dreams; those people put their trust in me and Charlie and Lew and Sweet.

Quiet, so only Sweet could hear me, I whispered "When I yell." Sweet nodded just enough that only I could see it.

I spoke. "I got the money. Right around my middle in a money belt." With both hands on the saddlehorn so the man wouldn't get jumpy, I moved the gray out in front.

"Well, well, well, well. A real cute idea. All right, sonny, if you got it, just keep your left hand on the saddlehorn and get it out slowly with your right."

I nodded and unbuttoned my big brown coat, then my shirt, and finally the middle of my long-handled underwear. I was moving slow, hoping they'd think I was scared to death. As I started to loosen the money belt, I just barely touched the spurs to the gray, reined him to the right, and moved slowly toward them. The blocky man brought the .44 around until it was pointing at me while his sidekick kept the shotgun on Charlie.

He let the gray take about two or three steps, then suddenly barked at me. "That's far enough! Just drop it on the ground right there."

I had to get closer. I kept my head down and pretended that I hadn't heard, that I was concentrating on the money belt. I nudged the gray enough to keep him walking slowly, closing the last ten feet a little at a time.

He opened his mouth to say something else and raised the .44 but I cut him off, trying to look and sound like I was cooperating. I pulled the money belt free and held it out by one end.

"Here it is," I said. For just a second he seemed to relax at the sight of what he figured was a fortune. I urged the gray in a walk straight toward his horse, leaning forward as if to offer him the money belt. I was less than five feet away when he raised the pistol and aimed it right at my chest. "That's far enough. Stop or . . ."

That's as far as he got.

I shrieked like a scalded mountain lion, whipped the money belt back along the flank of the gray, and jammed both spurs home. The big gray made the lunge of his life, broadside into the blocky man's horse. With the explosion of action the man threw his gun hand upward to protect himself. The gray knocked his horse clear over sideways into the thin man's horse, and we all went down in a tangle of screaming horses and arms and legs, amidst two shotgun blasts that went harmlessly into the air. The .44 went skittering off into the prairie dirt and grass, unfired. Sweet came charging in right behind me like a freight train.

I went clear over the blocky man's horse when the gray plowed into it, landing right in the middle of the scramble. When the thin man quit rolling I was right there waiting for him. I hit him in the face as hard as I could. He'd lost the shotgun when he went down, and all the fight went out of him. He threw both arms over his face, whimpering "Please mister, it was all his idea. Please don't hit me no more."

I jerked around to go back after the other one, but it was all over. Sweet had him unconscious on the ground and was standing over him, looking like he was almost begging him to try to get up. It hadn't lasted fifteen seconds.

I ran back to the gray, who was back on his feet. I'd gambled with the life of that big horse, and I'd never forgive myself if he was hurt. I swear he looked at me as if to say "That was a close one, boss, but we got it done." I checked his chest and legs and ankles just to be sure. Then I turned to Charlie and Lew, who were walking around gathering up the weapons, making sure neither robber would cause any further trouble.

"You two okay?" I asked.

"Yeah, we're fine. You?"

"I'm okay. I think the gray is too. Anybody get hit by the shotgun?"

Charlie shook his head. "No, it went into the air."

I picked up the money belt I'd dropped when the gray made his lunge and put it in my coat pocket. We tied the two men onto their horses and mounted up. Sweet had the shotgun, reloaded and cocked, leveled at the two renegades. Neither man had any doubt he'd blast them without blinking an eye if they so much as looked at him crooked. Lew was covering them with the .44.

As we started for Raymond I leaned forward in the saddle, whispering just loud enough for the gray to hear me. "You're pure horse." I knew if God sent good horses to heaven, some day that's where I would find the gray.

We stopped at the fork where I would angle west alone toward my home. "Mr. MacDonald, do you want me to go on into Raymond with you?"

He looked like he had expected the offer. "No, Henry, ye've done yer share and more. We're just a half hour from town. We'll get the money delivered. Yer folks are waiting. Head on home. And thank ye, fer all of us."

I felt a little embarrassed. I reached into my pocket. "Here's the money belt." I handed it to him and watched as he folded it and stuffed it inside his coat.

Unexpectedly a feeling crept up on the four of us at the same moment. We sat there and let it settle into our bones. It was finished! The desperate, make-it-or-break-it gamble had been won. We'd gone head to head with impossible odds and beat them. The feeling we shared for just that moment was precious beyond words. It belonged to us and the others in the crew forever. No one else. We'd paid the price and it was ours!

The horses, sensing they were nearly home, stirred and brought us back to reality.

"Mr. MacDonald, could I make a suggestion? When you find work for Phyllis Daniels, don't write to Billy. Write to Phyllis direct. Invite her out here yourself. Sometimes things like that come easier from someone other than your own father. If it all works out and she comes here, look for a chance to tell her about Fool's Hill. Tell her about getting Henry McEwen off Fool's Hill. About two days later she ought to figure it out."

Three weeks ago, I couldn't have said that to anyone, not even myself. Lew looked at Sweet and they both looked at the ground for a second, then back at me. Their faces were filled with silent respect. At that moment I felt a closeness to those three men that was rare and more precious to me than words can tell.

"I think yer right, Henry. I'll remember." Charlie raised his reins to start north.

"Mr. MacDonald, just one more thing. Anything you'd like me to tell my dad? I think I'll be spendin' some time just talkin' to him."

Charlie looked at me and I saw the beginnings of a smile tug at the corners of his mouth. "Yes, Henry. Tell yer father I'll be over to his place day after tomorrow to make an accounting of his cattle and deliver yer wages. And tell Jacob the cattle drive turned out fine. Everything was a success."

I looked him in the eyes as he spoke and I understood. I glanced at Sweet and Lew, and I think they understood the whole thing too. I raised my finger to my hat brim in a good-bye just as they did. I touched rein to the gray, turning him west for home, as the others pointed their mounts toward Raymond and tapped spur.

I arrived home as dusk was gathering. I reached down to slip the loop off my saddlehorn, unwrapping the thong that held Elmer's rawhide lariat in place. I dismounted with it in my hand, ground hitching the gray as the door of my home opened. Mother was wrapping a shawl over her shoulders as she walked out the door and started toward me. I could see Elmer still inside.

Mother came fast, talking as she came. "Henry, you're home, thank the Almighty. Are you all right? Did you get hurt?"

"I'm fine, mother. I'm fine."

She hesitated, sensing something new in me. Then, impulsively, she stepped in close and put her arms around me for just a minute, not wanting to embarrass me but unable to deny her mother's heart. I embraced her too. I could feel her stiffen with surprise and then relax, and we just stood there a moment and held each other.

I put my cheek against hers. "It's good to be home, mother. Is dad around?"

She stepped back with a look in her eyes like she didn't dare let herself hope. "He'll be along directly, Henry. He's just out at the pump thawing it for some house water. Come in; we'll freeze out here."

Inside, I handed Elmer his lariat. "Some day I'll find a way to pay you back for lendin' me this. A time or two it made all the difference in the world. Clark and I had to go into Sweetgrass to yank a great big old spotted maverick off the streets, and . . ."

I caught myself. "I'm getting ahead of myself. I'll tell you all about it later. I got a *lot* to tell you later. But right now there's things out there I should get inside, and I need to rub down the gray before I turn him to feed and water."

With Elmer helping, we finished in short order and returned to the house, him with my bedroll and me with the two packages. I started peeling the wrappings off the smaller box, explaining that the big package had to wait until Jacob came in.

First out of the box was the package for Elmer. He looked at me, surprised, then took it and started to tear the paper away.

The look on his face was priceless. He just stared and stared at the stainless steel bit. "Made by the Hereford Company out of

Texas," I said. "I think it's a pretty good one." I grinned a little as I spoke.

He didn't know what to say, or maybe he just couldn't talk right then. He just looked at me and back at the bit. That was enough for me.

I handed the long slender package to mother. When she got it undone and the comb dropped into her lap, she stopped still. Her eyes got moist and her voice wavered as she spoke. "It's beautiful, Henry. It's just beautiful." I grinned again. The pleasure it brought to her made me feel good, too.

At the sound of footsteps, we all turned toward the front door. That would be Jacob returning with the two house buckets full of water. I opened the door so he wouldn't have to set one of them down to open it himself. It took him a little by surprise.

"Better get in here before we all freeze, dad," I said as he started inside. He stopped stone still, and I know why. I hadn't called him dad for three years.

He walked to the kitchen sink, set the buckets down, and turned back, tugging at his gloves and his heavy coat.

"We heard some pretty wild stories from the crew that came back from Sweetgrass," he said. "You all right, Henry? You get hurt? We know about Fritz Hoffman. We attended the funeral."

"I'm fine. That was a sorry tragedy, about Fritz. How's his family?"

"We're all helpin' them on through the winter. Come spring Mrs. Hoffman will decide what she wants to do. She'll be all right."

I took his coat and hung it on the kitchen peg. "Yeah, there are some pretty wild stories to tell. Did you get the .45-70 back? Did the sorrel get back okay?"

"The sorrel is fine. We got the .45-70 back, along with a story that had to be a lie. Five hundred and eighty-two yards?"

I was grinning and he was trying not to.

"Lee Callister paced it off, so I don't know. I figure that wolf died of old age or a heart attack long before the bullet got there."

Elmer was starting to laugh. Dad grinned and then chuckled. Mother was smiling, watching all of it.

"I got something here for you." I reached for the tissue with the pocket knife and handed it to my father.

He was totally surprised. His cold, blocky hands worked at the paper until he found the knife. He held it in one hand, touching it gently with the other. Then he opened the blades, read "Solingen, Germany," and knew it was a good knife. He looked into my eyes and then carefully slipped it into his trouser pocket. "Thank you, Henry. Thank you."

"Dad, there's one more thing. It's for the family." I laid the big package on the kitchen table, motioning for them to open it. He and mother worked at it, stopping all motion when they saw the hard-shelled black banjo case. Slowly dad opened it, his eyes glistening as he stared at the banjo lying in the plush, red velvet case. No one moved or spoke for a long time. Then carefully, almost reverently, dad lifted it out of the case and ran his fingers over the strings. They weren't tuned, but he didn't seem to mind.

"Looks like we got some work to do, learnin' to play this. It'll be right nice havin' some music in the house." His voice was a little husky, his eyes a little too shiny.

Mother wiped at her eyes with her sleeve, trying to find something to cover up her tears. She stood quickly and walked over to the stove. "You men get yourselves washed and we'll get some supper on the table." Her voice sounded a little unsteady.

While we gathered up the paper and put things away, I told mother about the new clothes I'd bought in Chicago. Elmer and I set the table, and soon we sat down to some steaming hot beef and gravy, potatoes, and a little cabbage. Mother said grace and we started to eat.

"Charlie MacDonald said to tell you he'll be over day after tomorrow and make an accounting for your cattle. He'll pay my wages, too."

Father looked up at me.

I didn't wait. "Dad, there've been some real interesting things happened to me, and interesting people I've met. You probably heard some about the drive and Sweetgrass, but you haven't heard about Chicago. I never had a notion what it would be like to be there. I'm tellin' you, I never saw such a pile of people and cement and lights and automobiles."

Father looked interested in all of it and there was also something else in his expression—a kind of judging or gauging look. I remembered the last thing Charlie told me. "Oh, Mr. MacDonald said one other thing. He said to tell you the drive worked out fine. Everything was a success."

I looked my dad in the eyes as I said it and he knew what I meant. Quietly he spoke back to me. "I get the feeling Charlie was right." He looked at mother for a moment and something passed between them that made her stop and look down at her plate.

Dad reached for the potatoes. "About Chicago, Henry. Tell us about Chicago."

"Dad, it was the dangdest place. They have toilets right inside your hotel room that are half full of water and you pull a chain, and . . ."